Ag polit comm 5.00

THE FIVE LAWS of Liberty

Defending a Biblical View of Freedom

THE FIVE LAWS of Liberty

Defending a Biblical View of Freedom

Scott Hyland

The Five Laws of Liberty:
Defending a Biblical View of Freedom

Published by God and Country Press, an imprint of
AMG Publishers, Inc.
6815 Shallowford Rd.
Chattanooga, Tennessee 37421

ISBN 13: 978-0-89957-015-0
ISBN 10: 0-89957-015-1
First Printing—August 2010

Cover designed by Michael Largent at Indoor Graphics Corp., Chattanooga, TN

Interior design and typesetting by Reider Publishing Services, West Hollywood, California

Edited and proofread by Rebecca LuElla Miller and Rick Steele

Printed in Canada

15 14 13 12 11 10 –T– 7 6 5 4 3 2 1

To Jennifer,

My wife, my lover, my liberty, my sweetheart, my best friend

Other Books from God and Country Press

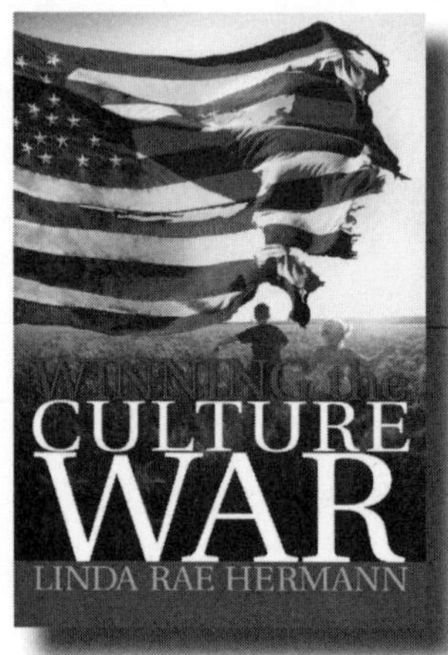

WINNING THE CULTURE WAR

Linda Rae Hermann

ISBN-13: 978-0-89957-025-9

http://www.WinningTheCultureWar.net

DEATH OF A CHRISTIAN NATION

Deborah Dewart, Attorney at Law

ISBN-13: 978-0-89957-023-5

http://www.DeathOfAChristianNation.com

For more information visit

www.GodAndCountryPress.com

or call 800-266-4977

ACKNOWLEDGMENTS

ANYONE WHO HAS EXPERIENCED the blessing of writing a book knows the time, effort, and patience that are required to bring it to publication. The final product is a collective effort—a cooperation of many people with a common vision. It is, therefore, with deepest gratitude that I thank the following people.

I want to thank, first of all, my heavenly Father for sending the ultimate example of liberty—His Son—Jesus Christ. He alone is the Author, Sustainer, and Finisher of true freedom.

God provided me with incredible parents who taught me as a child the basic principles of handling the great responsibility that comes along with the freedom we have been so abundantly blessed with in this great land. Thanks Mom and Dad.

I'm also grateful to my brothers—Jim, John, and Steve—who challenged me as a boy to be more than I was, who pushed me beyond what I would have been alone, and who continue to sharpen me as a man.

A special thank you to the entire team at AMG Publishers for standing as a light in the darkness. I could not have completed this project without the dedicated leadership of Rick Steele. His experience and guidance were invaluable to me. Thanks also to Becky Miller for strengthening and sharpening the overall message with the expertise of a well-seasoned copy editor. Kudos to Andrea Reider for her outstanding layout work. I am extremely encouraged that AMG remains a press committed to publish books that open the minds of our citizens to the truth of Jesus Christ.

I am grateful to the Founding Fathers of our country who were not only patriots in the truest sense of the word but also men who were committed to the teachings of Jesus Christ.

Thanks to Elizabeth Dalenberg, my friend and colleague, for the many hours that she dedicated to reading copy, editing, and helping me carve, sand, then polish my writing. This work would not have been possible without her.

To Dr. Ed Hindson, who is not only a real man of God but also a trusted mentor, thank you for encouraging me by providing opportunities to exercise my freedom of expression in print.

And to my loving wife, Jennifer, and to our three children—Scott, Matthew, and Abigail—you are my life and my liberty.

Contents

THE THIRD LAW OF LIBERTY: Respect Humanity

THE FOURTH LAW OF LIBERTY Control Yourself

THE FIFTH LAW OF LIBERTY: Protect and Serve Others

Foreword

BY MATHEW STAVER

DEAN AND PROFESSOR OF LAW
DIRECTOR, LIBERTY CENTER FOR LAW AND POLICY

The Declaration of Independence is one of the most significant documents in American history. What was a death warrant for Founders became the birth certificate for America and the liberty that would spread throughout the world.

Thomas Jefferson was the primary drafter of the Declaration, but the ideas contained therein were not unique to Jefferson. He referred to the document as "the reflection of the American mind." The concepts, and even many of the phrases contained in the Declaration, reflected the American mind because they were commonly held beliefs. The Declaration of Rights drafted by George Mason in Virginia shortly before the Declaration of Independence contained some of the same phrases and ideas. In fact, each aspect of the Declaration had been preached repeatedly by ministers from the pulpits.

While Jefferson may have added an elegant writing style to the Declaration of Independence, the substance was commonly shared among the Colonists. The Declaration begins with the common understanding that the Creator endowed each person with unalienable rights. These rights do not come from government or from the consent of the governed. They originate with God and are infused in each person because God created each one in His image. Government is not the author of these rights. If government is not the author, then government cannot take away these rights.

Government therefore has a singular duty according to the Founders—namely, government must protect these rights that originate from the Creator. Thus, civil servants, magistrates of the state—ministers of justice—have delegated duty to protect what God created.

The Declaration lists a few of the primary rights God infused in each human being. These include life, liberty, and the pursuit of happiness. The right to life is the right of all rights. Without life there is no liberty, and without liberty there can be no pursuit of happiness. A government that does not protect life will soon take your liberty, and when liberty is restricted, the pursuit of happiness vanishes. The right to own property means nothing to a corpse.

The revolutionary ideas contained in the Declaration of Independence gave birth to the most powerful, inventive, and free country in the world. America quickly became the most literate nation. How could this small band of foreign immigrants far exceed the achievements of their ancestors from across the pond? Why did the Revolution in America succeed while the simultaneous Revolution in France fail?

One easy answer to the last question is to compare the fundamental premises of the American Revolution with the French Revolution. The former spoke of life, liberty, and the pursuit of happiness. The latter spoke of liberty, fraternity, and equality. Life was absent from the French Revolution. Thus, the symbol of the French Revolution was the guillotine. The American Revolution begins with God.

The French Revolution begins with man and human reason. In the American Revolution, the place of government begins with the recognition that there is a God who created human beings, infused them with unalienable rights, and thus government's declared duty is to protect these rights.

In the French Revolution, there is government and only government. There is no God. Thus, rights come by the grace of the government. Government can bestow rights and government can take them away. This includes life. Those who dissent, well—they lose their head! That's why the guillotine became the symbol of the French Revolution.

The word "fraternity" encapsulated the French idea that rights come from the group. If the group decides your life is not worth saving, then your life is not worth saving. Since there was no higher authority than the group, the group was the supreme authority. There was no higher law to which earthly law must conform. Whatever the state said was the law no matter how arbitrary the rule may be.

But we come back to the earlier question. Where did the American revolutionaries get their ideas? They are expressed in the Declaration of Independence, but, as we said, the Declaration was a "reflection of the American mind." While the Founders read the classics, and read from the works of Montesquieu, John Locke, and Blackstone, the most commonly cited source by far was the Bible. In fact, the reason America became the most literate nation in the world was precisely because people were taught to read so they could read the Bible. The first compulsory education law in America was in the Colony of Massachusetts. It was called "The Old Deluder Satan Act." It was so named because Satan is a deceiver, and the best way to not be deceived is to read and understand the Scriptures. Thus, education was required to teach people how to read.

The Scripture teaches that God created Heaven and Earth. He created each person in His image. He is the Author of life. God establishes governments. He set up magistrates who have a fiduciary duty to the people to administer justice. Thus, there is a higher law. St. Augustine wrote that earthly laws must conform to higher law. Blackstone confirmed that if an earthly law does not conform to the higher law then it is no law at all. Blackstone was the source of law for anyone who became a lawyer during the Founding Era. In his "Letter from the Birmingham Jail," Martin Luther King, Jr. relied on higher law to defend why he obeyed some laws but not others. Laws that did not conform to God's higher law are no law at all and should not be obeyed.

If we are to have liberty, we must know the source of liberty. The source of liberty is not government. It is God. Government has a limited and prescribed duty—to protect this God-given liberty. Liberty begins with life. Without life there is no liberty, and without liberty there is no pursuit of happiness.

History is a good teacher. If we ignore history, we are doomed to repeat its mistakes. The history of the American and French Revolutions is illustrative of the two different philosophical foundations for government. One works while the other does not. One protects life while the other weighs life in a cost-benefit scale. One gives birth to liberty while the other devolves into tyranny.

Ideas have consequences. Today there are those who want us to forget our history. It is a powerful history indeed. Those who oppose liberty dislike the history of America. They either want us to forget it or to remake it. At the root of this effort lies the battle over worldviews. At the center of this battle is the place and existence of God. Without God, there is no freedom.

INTRODUCTION

ZEROING IN ON FREEDOM

TODAY MANY PEOPLE using the word *freedom* have little to do with acquiring or sustaining the state it represents. The word *freedom* launches from the silo of their soul and explodes into the atmosphere with the least amount of impact upon their lives or the lives of others. It has become nothing more than a word frivolously thrown into any sentence in order to excuse selfish behavior.

The Five Laws of Liberty is an honest examination of the biblical view of freedom. In Scripture, the word *freedom* is used no less than eighty-nine times in its various forms. Some of the most famous verses in all of Scripture have to do with freedom. Second Corinthians 3:17 boldly sets forth the proposition: "For the Lord is the Spirit, and wherever the Spirit of the Lord is, there is freedom" (NLT). Additionally, in Galatians 5:1, the Apostle Paul not only trumpets the decree that Christ set us free but also declares that freedom will only flourish as we keep standing firm in the faith.

If freedom can be found where the Lord is present, then in order to arrive at a proper understanding of freedom, we would serve ourselves best by studying His life. A thorough survey of the life of Christ makes it clear that He consistently took steps to preserve life. He did this by surrendering His freedom on behalf of others.

Jesus Christ demonstrated that the key to freedom was eternally linked to an intimate relationship with God. Everything that he did grew out of a deep desire to please His Father. Christ made it clear that a high view of God produces a high view of humanity, and this was certainly reflected in the way He treated the people within his sphere of influence. He not only displayed immortal perfection but also embraced and transformed the lives of the mortally imperfect. The preservation of life was the driving force behind his understanding of freedom.

Christ taught that freedom is the responsible pursuit and preservation of life. The practice of Christianity promotes freedom and preserves life better than any other system of belief. At least five laws of liberty can be observed from the life of Christ, and when these laws are followed, freedom flourishes for everyone. Tragically, when they are neglected, the most atrocious acts of violence are committed against humanity.

The chart below illustrates the five laws of liberty. When practiced, The Five Laws of Liberty promote freedom and preserve life. The Five Laws exist within the boundaries that God has set for humanity. In order for freedom to flourish within relationships, every action should be governed by The Five Laws of Liberty:

- *Remember* the Past
- Embrace the *Truth*
- *Respect* Humanity
- Restrain oneself (*Self-control*)
- *Protect and Serve* others

Life and liberty thrive within the parameters of The Five Laws of Liberty. As a nation, America proudly exhibits a heritage of practicing these laws. Unfortunately, in recent years we have witnessed deterioration of our focus on the founding principles of our country. If this tendency continues, our country will decline from democracy to anarchy, from anarchy to bondage, from bondage to tyranny, from tyranny to oppression, and from oppression to death. In order to preserve life and prevent the extinction of our nation, we must learn to train our sights upon **The Five Laws of Liberty**.

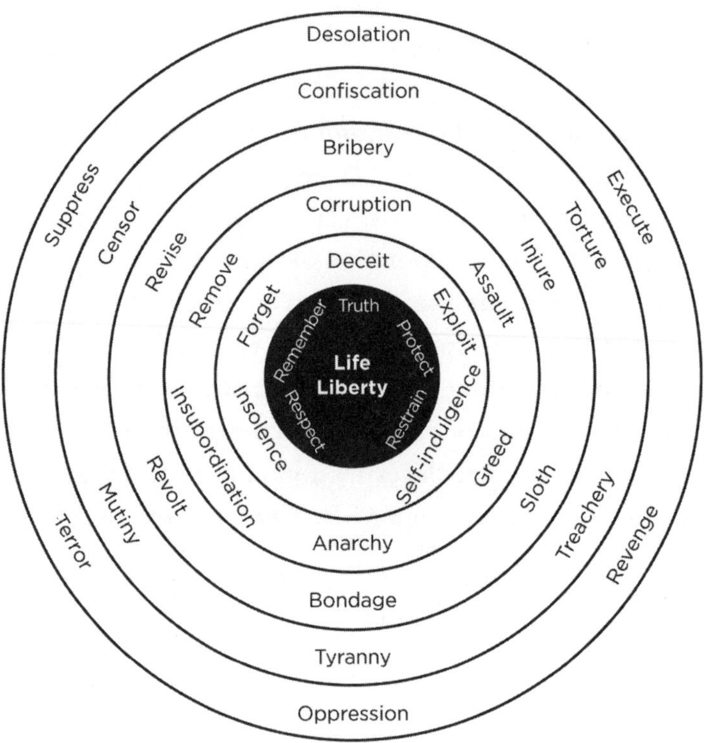

Desolation
Confiscation
Bribery
Corruption
Deceit
Truth
Life
Liberty
Suppress
Censor
Revise
Remove
Forget
Remember
Execute
Torture
Injure
Assault
Exploit
Protect
Respect
Restrain
Insolence
Insubordination
Revolt
Mutiny
Terror
Self-indulgence
Greed
Sloth
Treachery
Revenge
Anarchy
Bondage
Tyranny
Oppression

DEATH

THE FIRST LAW OF LIBERTY

Remember the Past

CHAPTER ONE

The Fireworks of Freedom

WHY IT IS IMPORTANT TO HAVE A PROPER UNDERSTANDING OF FREEDOM

Freedom is one of those words that is easy to say but difficult to explain. People refer to freedom frequently but may not really know what it means. A brief glance at some of the statements people make concerning freedom should cause us to question their understanding.

The terms *freedom* or *free* are often misused in declarations such as "Freedom is my right!" or "This is a free country; I can do whatever I want to do!" or "You can't tell me what to do, this is a free country!"

Is freedom really a right? Does true freedom equal doing whatever an individual wants to do? Exactly what does a person mean by saying, "This is a free country"? Does such a statement imply that since we live in a free society, one person cannot tell another person what to do? And if one cannot tell another person what to do, is that not itself a restraint upon freedom?

All facetiousness aside, one can see that flaws exist in such declarations. We must first understand that freedom is a precious commodity; otherwise, arriving at a proper understanding of it will be impossible. Freedom is not something to be taken lightly. Nor is it a term to be frivolously thrown into any sentence so that one can get his own way. By using the word *freedom*, a person does not automatically trump all other arguments against his position. Arguably the ease with which a person tosses a term around directly correlates to the value that person places upon the term. Therefore we have to ask ourselves the question, "Do we value freedom the way we value Grandmother's fine china, or do we treat it like something as common as Tupperware®?"

The fact is that *freedom* is a sacred word, and it should not be considered common. Freedom should be to Americans what fireworks are to the Fourth of July. People do not hear them very often, but when they do, childhood memories flood their minds. They contemplate nostalgic thoughts of the price others paid for the current liberties they enjoy. Every exploding canister echoes the sounds of historical battlefields all over this great nation.

FREEDOM IS A PRIVILEGE

The Value of a Privilege

Unfortunately those who use the term *freedom* most frequently have little to do with acquiring it or sustaining it. An American POW in a Hanoi Hilton cell inscribed these words on the wall: "Freedom has a taste to those who fight and die for it that the protected will never know."[1] Many veterans have been disheartened by the way in which some citizens flippantly spend the freedom soldiers purchased for them. When people use the terms "*freedom*" and "*right*" interchangeably in front of soldiers, those men may relive the wounds of battle. You can see the anguish on their faces and hear the breath of life expelled from their lungs as they try to convince themselves that their ears are deceiving them.

Nevertheless, their ears are not deceiving them. Many people do think that words like *freedom* and *right* are compatible. For example, they will say things such as, "It is my right to have healthcare provided to me at the government's expense!" Or, "It is my right as an American citizen to make a decent wage." Granted, everyone wants to be taken care of in one way or another, but are we to demand free healthcare or a higher wage from the government? Frankly, these two examples demonstrate how demanding people can become when the focus is shifted from freedom to finances.

Quite honestly, freedom is not something that can be demanded, especially financial freedom. In the past, most parents taught their children that benefits such as healthcare and a decent wage were earned through thrift and hard work. The more diligently a person worked, the more opportunities he would create. A good work ethic would also encourage an employer to commit to the employee by providing benefits that were earned. One of those benefits, in addition to an increase in salary, may be provisional health insurance.

This concept is certainly not new. In fact, this kind of arrangement is what most Americans used to mean when they made statements about the American Dream. Our history is full of individuals who took advantage of a free economic system and made something of themselves.

Indeed, Abraham Lincoln, one of the greatest Presidents to occupy the Oval Office, believed in this work ethic. He did not believe the government owed any man anything except an environment that allowed him to freely pursue financial ventures at his own expense. This belief is one reason President Lincoln fought against slavery. Slavery obligated others to pay for the entrepreneurial pursuits of a few. He believed that slavery suffocated individual opportunity for economic freedom. David Donald in his book, *Lincoln*, states the following:

> he firmly adhered to the labor theory of value: "labor is the source from which human wants are mainly supplied." Labor was thus "prior to, and independent of, capital"; indeed "capital is the fruit of labor, and could never have existed if labor had not first existed." But capital, though derivative, performed a valuable service in a free society, because those who had it could offer employment to "the prudent, penniless beginner in the world" who owned "nothing save two strong hands that God has given him, [and] a heart willing to labor." If this novice worked industriously and behaved soberly, he could in a year or two save enough to buy land for himself, to settle, marry, and beget sons and daughters, and presently he, too, would begin employing other laborers.[2]

A proper understanding of financial freedom is obviously only one aspect of freedom overall, but it is a good place to open up a discussion on the topic because there are so many citizens, especially the young, who are unschooled in the way of freedom. Parents who have acquired a comfortable lifestyle with a decent wage owe it to their children to teach them how they arrived at that point. Our nation was built upon the idea that if a person wants liberty, especially financial liberty, he is to go out and work as hard he can. The government's only responsibility in this matter is to provide a safe environment in which such work can be attempted. History has shown that a man who is free to generate his own wealth will generate more wealth than a man who is not free. Our country has traditionally referred to this as the freedom of commerce.

Therefore a free country with free commerce beckons physically resilient individuals to put forth a valiant, working effort in order to achieve financial liberty. After they have given all they can, they need to give some more. Then and only then may their diligence be recognized favorably by someone else who can use what they have to offer. That kind of grit does not come from the tongue; that kind of grit comes from getting things done.

The older generation is doing a poor job of communicating this work ethic to the next generation. Teaching responsibility takes place by giving a person responsibilities. It is something that has to be taught at a very young age. A young person who is not given responsibilities, or who is not expected to behave responsibly, tends to be irresponsible. Since more material goods for less effort have been given to the children of this generation as opposed to previous generations, these young people expect more for less.

In the same way, our society has neglected to require a valiant effort before a reward is granted; we have also neglected to expect this generation of Americans to learn how to maintain our foundational principles. In other words, in the same way that we have failed to teach financial principles, we have also failed to teach foundational principles. As a result, we have ended up with people who are not only financially spoiled but who are enjoying the spoils of freedom like gluttons—ones who are too selfish to preserve any staples for the next generation.

Consequently, our country distances itself from its past with each passing year as if we are ashamed of the behavior of our past. This development is confusing because our past is the very vessel that has carried us to our present.

The same complication faces us when our nation goes to war against an aggressor. Protestors tend to materialize from nowhere. They enjoy the freedom that was won for them in the past, but they neglect their responsibility to maintain and defend it today.

So what do they do? They go to a local retailer to buy some supplies. After they have reached for their wallet and removed American dollars, they congregate together. Then with a military orderliness, they hold up their poster boards and march in unison while chanting the mantras of freedom as they oppose the war. What they fail to recognize is how many liberties, purchased during previous wars, they have exercised. In this scenario alone, they have exercised the freedom to exchange goods and services. They have also exercised the liberty to peaceably assemble. Finally, the one that they have exercised the most but know about the least, they have exercised their freedom of expression.

THE DEFINITION OF *PRIVILEGE*

Clearly freedom is not a right but a privilege. But what is a privilege? There is something deep and rich about the word *privilege*. The best way to understand what a person means by the word *privilege* is to analyze its use in daily life and then to illustrate it.

A person might say, "It has been a privilege serving you today." Alternatively, after being thanked for accompanying someone in a task, a person may respond, "The privilege was all mine." A privilege has much to do with a partnership and the way each party views itself. A privilege may be granted by a higher authority, but oftentimes, especially within the realm of social behavior, this concept has a lot to do with the view of oneself. If a person humbly esteems others as better than himself, he will consider many interactions a privilege that others would not.

Many of the privileges that we enjoy as a society are granted or guarded by a higher authority; take for instance driving. In order to drive in any state, an individual must qualify. First he has to be of legal age. Then he has to apply for a permit that will only allow him to drive at certain times with another licensed adult. After a certain period, usually two to six months, he may then attempt to pass a driver's examination during which he will be required to show competency, both in theory and in practical execution, to an officer of the state. If he satisfies the licensing official, then and only then is he granted a license to drive.

The word *license* certainly is an understandable term, but it is a bit peculiar and misleading because it is a license issued or granted by the state. If a fledgling driver should decide to disobey the laws of the state, he will not enjoy his license very long; for the very state that granted his license also has the authority to guard its citizens from negligent and reckless individuals. Consequently, it would be appropriate to understand this license to drive as a privilege, not as a right.

In order to more firmly grasp the concept of a privilege, it is imperative to probe into why any state has authority to issue a license or to permit any similar benefit. The state has been given this authority to grant other agencies or individuals limited authority. The Constitution governs the states within the United States. Any constitution is only as strong as the men who abide by it—meaning that the weight of a given constitution is correlated to the value which any generation of governing officials wishes to bestow upon it. People, not paper, govern states. If the elected leaders decide to make laws overriding a state's original constitution, they can do so without the least bit of backtalk from the constitution because paper does not talk. The question then becomes, how do we produce men who will govern with the original principles that this country was founded upon?

THE FUTILITY IN DECLARING FREEDOM TO BE A RIGHT

Declaring freedom to be a right will swiftly prove to be inadequate. The notion of freedom as a right can easily be challenged. Certainly some people hold to the belief that "freedom is a right." However, freedom as a right cannot be maintained unless some citizens are willing to give up some rights. If an American soldier during World War II laid down his weapon on the beaches of Normandy and threw up his arms screaming, "In my beloved country, freedom is a right!" he would have been hewn in pieces by the barrage of metal flying toward him. During wartime only a lunatic would expect his rights to be honored in another country.

Given the right set of circumstances, one human being could appeal to another human being through rational diplomacy. However, an appeal to rationality requires both parties to agree upon that which is rational. The only other time that a reasonable appeal can be made is when the stronger party in a negotiation is rational. If the stronger party or the higher authority of any negotiation wishes to concede to the request of a weaker party, it may do so. However, it would be considered ridiculous for the weaker party to declare its will as if it were in control of the negotiations.

Family politics are very useful in a discussion concerning freedom for they allow a person to understand the larger political arena better.

A four-year-old boy may ask his father on the way to the toy store if he can drive the new family van, but a rational father would not concede to such a request. First of all, it is against the law for little boys to drive automobiles (even though some men drive like little boys). Secondly, conceding to such a request would endanger the lives of not only the little boy and his father but also everyone within proximity of the van. This request must not be fulfilled no matter how persistent and assertive the child becomes. However, if while exiting the toy store, the four-year-old asks his father for fifty cents so that he can drive the stationary vehicle at the front of the store, it would be perfectly reasonable and within the power of the father to grant such a request.

Some no doubt may argue that negotiating within a family is not always handled as neatly and properly as it was in the example of the preceding paragraph. Many parents today make unreasonable concessions to their children. Some parents do this because they do not have the volition to deny their child's request; others do it simply to stop their children from squawking. However, parents who fill unreasonable requests not only end up with spoiled children but also limit their personal freedom within the family as well as within society. We must teach our children through our words and our actions that freedom is a privilege to be granted and not a right to be demanded.

CHAPTER TWO

The Revolution of Responsibility

WITH PRIVILEGE COMES RESPONSIBILITY

Recognizing the truth about privilege is only a start. We must also teach others, especially the young that *with privilege comes responsibility*. If an individual desires more freedom, then he must demonstrate that he can handle the freedom he currently enjoys. "Why does it have to be this way?" Before this question can be answered, we must consider the origin of responsibility.

Where does responsibility come from? Does a person wake up one morning and have responsibility bestowed upon him? Or do we come to expect older children and grown-ups to behave responsibly as if they acquired it through osmosis or conformed to it because of peer pressure? These are questions that must be answered in order to arrive at a proper understanding of responsibility.

Responsibility is something that must be taught. Lessons regarding responsible behavior should begin when a child is very young. Parents actually have to teach their children the responsibility of being kind to others. In fact, they have to teach all of the responsibilities that will necessitate a healthy social existence throughout the life of the child. As a child learns to behave in certain areas, he will have to develop responsible behavior in other areas as well. Sharing, for example, is one of the most basic lessons in responsibility that every child should be taught. When a child is taught to share, he should simultaneously be taught to speak in a civil manner to others by using words such as *please* and *thank you*.

Therefore, when a child is taught to share, he also learns the benefit of good manners and proper communication. Additionally, through sharing, a child is taught good stewardship of his time and property.

Take, for example, a little girl who is playing with a doll that she received as a gift on her birthday from her mother. One day her mom allows her to invite a friend over to play. Of course, when her friend comes over, she sees many other dollies, but she would like to hold the one that the little girl is showering so much attention upon. A little girl who has been taught to be kind may even notice the longing eyes of her friend and volunteer to share her doll. The key concept is "voluntarily." When children finally learn to share out of sincerity rather than compulsion, it is one of the most beautiful acts of responsible behavior.

Conversely we have all been exposed to those instances when children are not so kind to each other, especially when their favorite toys become the focus of other children's attention. Child's play between friends can very quickly erupt into all-out war, thus illustrating the basic tendencies in all of us to revert to selfishness and irresponsibility. If selfishness and irresponsibility were not innate tendencies, then we would not have to be taught unselfishness and responsibility.

Sharing not only becomes a responsibility but also a way in which responsibility is taught. If a child is never taught to voluntarily share his property, he will not be prone to share as an adult. If a child is never given responsibility, he will inevitably become irresponsible. Thus the only thing that he will learn is how to waste both the time and resources of his family. He may even squander valuable friendships.

Therefore, parents should keep responsibility high on their list of traits to teach their offspring. Every good parent wants to rear responsible children. But in order for this development to take place, parents must model responsibility throughout the day. Daily tasks such as cleaning up the dishes or taking out the trash should be done in the presence of youngsters. When children are old enough, they too can participate in the family responsibilities. If children take part in consuming the benefits that come from being a part of the family, then they should also take part in the essential chores that produce those benefits.

Once the child can interpret, comprehend, and understand instructions as basic as putting away his toys, he should be given responsibilities. This will not only make the child feel good about himself, but it will also alleviate some of the pressures upon Mom and Dad and free them to dedicate their time to some other task. When parents teach their children to be responsible, they themselves are behaving responsibly by producing responsible citizens who will one day participate responsibly within society. This will not only contribute to the freedom of the family but also to the society at large.

THE CONTEMPORARY UNDERSTANDING OF RESPONSIBILITY

Unfortunately a brief glance at our society demonstrates that an epidemic of irresponsibility has spread across the land. There are people in our society who promote the idea that a person should be able to act as irresponsibly as he wants, and in the end, he can hold others responsible for his mistakes and messes. Kathleen Parker, a columnist with the *Orlando Sentinel*, recently wrote an article titled, "Eat, drink and sue." She states that people knowingly use tobacco and consume alcoholic beverages even though they have been warned repeatedly about the negative effects of such products. She concludes that a major part of the blame for this behavior should rest upon the shoulders of the lawyers who represent irresponsible clients, finding others at fault for the consequences of their choices. She states, "Litigiousness appears to be a disease of near-plague proportions. Can't hack your life? Blame someone else, hire a lawyer and retire early."[3]

In many instances today, if an individual has a problem, he can first turn to someone else to affix the blame; then he can also come to expect someone else to be responsible for fixing the problem. Many people today act in a selfish and irresponsible manner and then blame everyone from God to the devil, from parents to strangers, and from friends to enemies.

Today a person can even blame nature when there is no one else to blame.

THE TRUE MEANING OF RESPONSIBILITY

Someone somewhere must step forward and accept the consequences for actions. We are told that for every action, there is an opposite and equal reaction; actions bring about consequences, how an individual personally responds to a consequence is a true measure of responsibility. When a person is involved in an act that causes harm, discomfort, or inconvenience, that person should be held liable. We often refer to holding a person accountable as justice or fair play. Such evenhandedness seems as though it should be common practice; however, in our society justice is oftentimes held up by litigation or eliminated by excuses.

Therefore, at least three questions need to be asked:

- When should an individual be held responsible for his actions?
- When are other people held responsible?
- How does a person weigh a matter to distinguish which party should be held more accountable when someone has acted irresponsibly?

Answering these questions can be difficult at times, but they will help in determining a person's understanding of freedom and responsibility. How do these questions relate to, promote, or detract from freedom? We are going to begin with the basic unit in the society, the individual.

Does one individual in a society of over three hundred million people really affect the whole? C. S. Lewis in his book *Mere Christianity* answers this question marvelously by setting forth an illustration of a fleet of ships on an ocean. This fleet represents society as a whole. As long as each pilot continues to move along with the fleet in an orderly and organized fashion, the whole fleet operates in freedom. If an individual pilot were to intentionally ram his ship into a neighboring ship, that would detract from freedom. As a result, he would be liable for the restoration of freedom to all parties. Most people would agree that if an individual intentionally assaults somebody else, that individual should be held liable for punitive damages.

However, C. S. Lewis continues that there are some pilots who would attempt to argue that as long as they are operating their own ships, it should not matter what they do or neglect to do. He then demonstrates how ridiculous this type of thinking is by explaining that if an individual pilot neglects the maintenance of his ship, and his engine seizes or his rudder gets stuck, it is likely that his ship will collide with another in the fleet.[4] This demonstrates once again how an irresponsible person actually robs the responsible person of his freedoms.

At the same time, this illustration also defeats the idea that a person can act as irresponsibly as he wants as long as he is not hurting anybody else. The truth is that an individual gives up the control over his consequences when he acts with negligence and irresponsibility, whether or not he is alone or in the company of others. Furthermore, there is no guarantee that his actions will not affect others. More often than not, careless and selfish attitudes do not accomplish anything but pain, suffering, and bondage for others.

Therefore, in order for freedom to exist for the maximum benefit to all, all must act in a responsible manner. Responsibility should be understood as the act of governing self for the benefit of others. Negligence should then be viewed as the act of destroying self to the detriment of others. Responsibility is our response to those within our scope of influence. The primary element of this response should be composure and self-control at all times. These traits, in turn, will not only benefit others but oneself as well. A responsible individual will actually promote self through promoting others. An irresponsible individual will demote himself while simultaneously pulling down others.

Since it is not only idealistic but also unrealistic to think that all citizens within a society will act responsibly at all times, it must also be understood that the moment a person carelessly behaves, other people, who truly understand freedom will take the responsibility of holding him accountable for his behavior. One can only hope when this happens that the person who seizes control will be someone who would treat us in a manner in which he would want to be treated.[5]

If freedom is to continue to exist for the majority, then responsible citizens must be willing to get involved when others are behaving irresponsibly. Responsible citizens can and should assist irresponsible individuals, but the assistance should come in the form of aid and instruction that would enable them to behave responsibly in the future. In order to do this, responsible citizens must be willing to hold the irresponsible to a high standard of accountability. If numerous attempts to help have been met with resistance, then there has to come a time when penalties should be leveled against the irresponsible citizen, depending upon the severity of his negligence.

Clearly responsibility extends beyond an individual being accountable for the actions of self. It must include helping others who are in distress, whether they recognize it or not.[6] Obviously our first duty within a free society is to fulfill our own obligations. However our second duty is to make sure that others are fulfilling their obligations as well. If we fail to do so, eventually the freedom that we enjoy as individuals will erode. This erosion will be the result of neglected responsibility, and everybody within the society in some way or another pays for negligence. Therefore it is in our best interests to hold others, as well as ourselves, to a high standard of accountability. What standard should we follow?

The standard that we decide to follow has to be completely fair for every individual. It would be impossible to customize an objective system based upon individual preference. Therefore fairness will only flourish for all individuals within a society that truly understands freedom is a privilege that comes with certain responsibilities. In our society, we have come to expect that all individuals should be afforded the dignity that comes from being human. Therefore we believe that all human beings, whether they control themselves or not, should be treated in a just and fair manner. There has to be a reason why we, as a society, place so much emphasis upon the fair treatment of individuals.

Our society places a major emphasis upon the fair treatment of individuals because people are valuable regardless of their physiological conditions, socioeconomic background, utility, or past behavior. Human beings derive intrinsic value from somewhere. Where exactly does this value originate? If this standard or value changes over time, then human value will be driven by the cultural forces of the day. If human value is driven by fickle standards that change like the direction of the wind, then some humans will be seen as more valuable than others simply because of what they do. Human beings have to be viewed as more than just a commodity based upon utility.

How do we avoid basing human value upon utility? The answer has to come from outside of humanity. There has to be a commitment to a higher ideology. If humans determine human value, then it is possible for humans in positions of power to take advantage of those who are powerless. However, if human value is determined by something higher than humanity, then we may be able to tap into something that determines the value of each individual more objectively. The objective standard that determines the universal value for each individual may be discovered through fulfilling certain responsibilities. A strong dedication to humanity will increase the worth of each individual. There still has to be something or someone who holds us accountable to this strong dedication to each other, regardless of our background.

THE FOUNDATION OF FREEDOM

Having thoroughly dealt with the meaning of responsibility, it now becomes important to examine the duties that freedom necessitates. In no way is the following intended to be a comprehensive list. These duties or responsibilities should be viewed more as fundamentals, or pillars of freedom. The foundation that rests beneath the feet of these pillars was not established *by us* but rather *for us*. That foundation was intended to be established as an immovable rock that was anchored, not by forms that were fashioned with wood and fastened by nails, but rather by forms that were created from the minds of men and fastened by the conviction of a commitment to a higher ideology. It is impossible to discuss the foundation of freedom without also addressing the responsibilities of freedom, which are the five laws of liberty.

THE FIRST LAW OF LIBERTY IS TO REMEMBER THE PAST

The men responsible for conceiving the foundation of our nation, and the men who we must never forget, are referred to as the Founding Fathers of the United States of America. The ideology they consistently adhered to, agreed upon, and affirmed was the driving force behind their high and lofty achievements. This ideology or philosophy was a belief in and accountability to a higher authority. Evidence of this fact is displayed with much emphasis in every one of the official documents upon which this nation was conceived; this higher authority is referred to by such terms as *Nature's God*, *our Creator*, Supreme Judge and/or *our Lord*.

Among the Founding Fathers, there was unanimous and mutual consent that their utter dependence for sustenance and survival was "… with a firm reliance on the protection of Divine Providence."[7] As a result, two of the most solid legal documents ever to be forged in the minds of men, were written and then ratified. Those two documents were The Declaration of Independence and The Constitution of the United States. Many would argue that these documents are unrivaled by any other nation's constitution.

What is it that makes the Constitution of the United States superior to every other governing document in the world? One of the most obvious distinctions that our forefathers made was not only the idea of a government of the people, by the people, and for the people, but also that a free government such as ours could only be guaranteed as the people took the responsibility of guarding and defending their liberties. The people guarantee liberty. The citizens of the new nation were a group of people who understood a unified commitment to a higher cause. John Adams described in detail the type of people for whom our government was established:

> We have no government armed with power capable of contending with human passions unbridled by morality and religion. Avarice, ambition, revenge, or gallantry, would break the strongest cords of our Constitution as a whale goes through a net. Our Constitution was made only for a moral and religious people. It is wholly inadequate to the government of any other.[8]

John Adams recognized what many of us fail to acknowledge today—that it is not the Constitution that keeps the people, but the people who keep the Constitution. Even that is a choice. Apart from the people, and not just any people but a "moral and religious people," the Constitution is just another fading document. If the people choose not to keep the Constitution, then our government will no longer look as our forefathers envisioned. This reality should alarm all freedom-loving Americans today, especially because the Founding Fathers conceived of our representative government in the midst of tyranny. They saw tyranny firsthand and solved the problems it presented. They were not looking back at history as we are today. History was looking at them right in the face, and none of them even blinked. They understood their enemy and how to defeat him. Concurrently then, while giving birth to a nation, they also protected against its demise.

Even though our nation had been established as one that would be governed by the majority, our forefathers foresaw that the only way to maintain the freedoms that had been won was to set up safeguards for the individual. These safeguards came in the form of the first ten Amendments to the Constitution. We call these individual safeguards the Bill of Rights.

What did our forefathers see that caused them to place so much stress upon guarding the freedoms won in the Revolutionary War? They had secured their independence from a religiously oppressive government. This oppression came in the form of the suppression of Christian denominations opposed to the state denomination in England. One can conclude that the Founding Fathers acted as they did because they experienced governmental restriction and suppression of individual liberties, especially religious ones. Therefore, within three years of ratifying the Constitution, our forefathers formulated the Bill of Rights for the individual.

One can see the intention of the Founding Fathers in these Amendments. A progressive and sequential order exists in the Bill of Rights. As intentional as these men were in everything else that they did in establishing our government, arguably the placement of an Amendment was equally strategic. In fact each particular Amendment actually served to guarantee the stability of the Amendment that followed. The complexity of the order of the original Amendments is so deep that it can also be argued that each one guarded the one that preceded. If the previous Amendment was taken away, then, by default, the next would topple. At the same time, in order to take by force one of these individual liberties, all would have to be countered.

The construction of the Constitution then can be likened to the construction of a building, evidenced in the following statement by Benjamin Franklin at the Continental Convention addressing George Washington, the President of the Convention:

> I have lived, Sir, a long time, and the longer I live, the more convincing proofs I see of this truth that God governs in the affairs of men .... We have been assured, Sir, in the sacred writings, that "except the Lord build the house they labor in vain that build it." I firmly believe this; and I also believe that without his concurring aid we shall succeed in this political building no better, than the builders of Babel: We shall be divided by our little partial local interests; our projects will be confounded, and we ourselves shall become a reproach.[9]

Although this statement was made before the Bill of Rights was published, an onlooker can already see, in seminal form, the wisdom of appealing to a higher authority for the construction of this "political building." In other words, what Benjamin Franklin was saying was that in order for successful construction of this new government to take place, all of the individual participants or builders had to be looking for guidance from an agreed upon higher authority. Not just any higher authority, but rather the one identified in the sacred writings, namely the New Testament.

Therefore, the Founding Fathers understood that in order for individual and collective success to take place, the nation had to realize that individual liberties could be guaranteed only as long as divine principles were upheld. Just like a building, the individual part depended upon the unity of the whole; the unity of the whole depended upon the integrity of the part.[10]

Clearly, our forefathers' darkest fears can be realized simply by attack on the protections set forth in the Bill of Rights.

The Bill of Rights is not just a wish list; it is a "rights" list that only exists as the laws of the higher authority are enforced. These men knew that the formation of these rights had been a long and arduous process. They knew exactly what they had and what they would have to fight for.

The First Amendment states the basic rights: "Congress shall make no law respecting an establishment of religion, or prohibiting the free exercise thereof; or abridging the freedom of speech, or of the press; or the right of the people peaceably to assemble, and to petition the Government for a redress of grievances."[11]

The framers of the Constitution also knew that these rights must be defended; thus they added the Second Amendment, which guarantees the right to bear arms and to form a well-regulated militia. At the same time, the safeguards contained within the First Amendment act as a shield guaranteeing the rights of the Second.

This intertwining was not only limited to the Bill of Rights, however. Our Founding Fathers maintained this mentality at every level with each new document they wrote. They did not conceive the Bill of Rights without the seed of the Constitution. Furthermore, they did not conceive the Constitution apart from the seed of the Declaration of Independence. These were not test tube documents conjured up in some vacuum apart from history. They were, indeed, the result of history that bred deep-felt convictions. As far removed as Abraham Lincoln was from the Declaration, he still referred to it with veneration. In fact, David Herbert Donald, one of the foremost authorities today on the life of Lincoln, recognized that when Lincoln gave his Gettysburg Address he was

> reminding his listeners—and, beyond them, the thousands who would read his words—that theirs was a nation pledged not merely to constitutional liberty but to human equality.... In language that evoked images of generation and birth— using what the Democratic *New York World* caustically called "obstetric analogies"—he stressed the role of the Declaration in the origins of the nation, which had been "conceived in Liberty" and "brought forth" by the attending Founding Fathers.[12]

Not only were these documents conceived within history, they have a longstanding ancestry of their own. For instance,

The Mayflower Compact gave birth to the Fundamentals of Connecticut. The Fundamentals of Connecticut gave birth to the New England Confederation. The New England Confederation gave birth to the Rights of the Colonists, written by Samuel Adams, also known as the Father of the Revolution. The Rights of the Colonists gave birth to the Declaration of Independence. The Declaration of Independence gave birth to the Constitution. And the Constitution gave birth to the Bill of Rights.

One cannot understand any of these documents unless he understands the progressive influence of each. A document that has descended from a previous document out of necessity contains within it elements from which it came. This progression should not be difficult to understand, especially if a person compares the way in which children relate genetically to their parents. In a similar way, the cumulative influence of one historical document upon another leaves sort of a genetic print upon the next. Language is a code by which humans communicate, and when the written word comes into contact with human history, amazing documents can come into being as truth is accurately communicated.

Where then did each of the preceding documents derive their core values? If each one of them contains shared organic material, then it would logically follow that it is possible to trace the lineage of these documents back to a source document. What follows is the core of each one of the five documents leading to the Constitution. Today we might refer to these distilled assertions as purpose or mission statements. The *Mayflower Compact* states the following: "Having undertaken for the Glory of God, and Advancement of the

Christian Faith … a Voyage to plant the first colony in the northern Parts of Virginia … [we] combine ourselves together into a civil Body Politick, for … Furtherance of the Ends aforesaid."[13]

The Fundamentals of Connecticut even more specifically delineates its core purpose in the following:

> Enter into combination and confederation together, to maintain and preserve the liberty and purity of the gospel of our Lord Jesus which we now profess …. Which, according to the truth of the said Gospel, is now practiced amongst us; as also, in our civil affairs to be guided and governed according to such laws, rules, orders, and decrees.[14]

The New England Confederation, in which the state of Connecticut also participated, was formed just four years after the Fundamentals of Connecticut had been ratified, and declared, "We all came into these parts of America, with one and the same end and aim, namely, to advance the Kingdom of our Lord Jesus Christ."[15] As it was noted earlier, Samuel Adams is not only considered the Father of the Revolution but he also authored "The Rights of the Colonists." What did he decree to be the core values, the genetic ancestor, the very essence of authority by which the colonists were granted these rights? "These may be best understood by reading and carefully studying the institutes of the great Law Giver and Head of the Christian Church, which are to be found clearly written and promulgated in the New Testament."[16]Samuel Adams decrees in plain language that the source of these rights is none other than the Divine Lawgiver found within the pages of the New Testament.

Finally, the Declaration of Independence itself proudly displays its heritage by referring to its source with such comments as "the Laws of Nature and of Nature's God … that all men are created equal, that they are endowed by their Creator with certain unalienable Rights … appealing to the Supreme Judge of the world for the rectitude of our intentions … with a firm reliance on the protection of Divine Providence…."[17] In addition to this neon display within the Declaration, fifty of the fifty-six signers of the Declaration belonged to Christian denominations.[18]

Therefore, it is patently obvious that the commonly shared predecessor of all of these amazing documents was none other than the New Testament itself. People who disagree with this well-established fact either have never fully exposed themselves to a broad sampling of the history of the United States of America, which makes them ignorant of their own heritage, or they just choose to ignore their heritage and tread their own paths, which makes them ungrateful to the very ideals and sacrificial actions that have provided for them not only the most prosperous nation in the history of mankind, but also the very vehicle which granted them the freedom to pursue their own interests.

Of the five documents from which the above samples were taken, only two remain—the Constitution and the Bill of Rights. Certainly some people might argue that there is no specific language within the Constitution to support the idea that our governing document was directly or indirectly influenced by the New Testament. Some may concede that there were men who participated in the forging of the document who had Christian convictions. They may also allow that some of those men's convictions may have trickled down into the proceedings. Nevertheless, some would argue that the overall body of the Constitutional Convention was scrupulous in restraining any specific language that would expose the Constitution to a Christian label.

In response to such a statement, we must place this question before history: Is there any historical documentation that unequivocally aligns the Constitution with Christianity? One such document from a Senate Judiciary Committee dated January 19, 1853, states the following:

> In the law, Sunday is a "dies non;".... The executive departments, the public establishments, are all closed on Sundays; on that day neither House of Congress sits.... Here is recognition by law, and by universal usage, not only of a Sabbath, but of the Christian Sabbath, in exclusion of the Jewish or Mohammedan Sabbath.... The recognition of the Christian Sabbath [by the Constitution] is complete and perfect.[19]

What's more, as stated previously, the Constitution descended from a heavily saturated Christian line. Not finding overt Christian language within the document, as we have already seen, does not automatically disqualify it from having a Christian heritage. Besides this fact, it must be kept in mind that the reason we have a Constitution of the United States was because our forefathers declared their independence from England. Therefore, The Declaration of Independence is our charter and is the very place that citizens should find explicit Christian wording. If the Constitution is not the charter, where then does that leave the document in the scheme of our history? The Constitution should be seen as the vehicle or the by-laws of the charter, as stated so eloquently by Tim LaHaye:

> The Declaration of the United States is our Charter. It is the legal document that made us a nation like all the other nations of the world. It doesn't tell us how we are going to run our country—that is what our Constitution does. In a corporation, the Charter is higher than the By-laws and the By-laws must be interpreted to be in agreement with the Charter. Therefore, the Constitution of the United States must be in agreement with the Declaration of the United States (more commonly known as the Declaration of Independence). The most important statement in our Declaration is that we want to operate under the laws of God. Why is all of this so important? Because today, when the courts are deciding what the Constitution means, they should remember our Charter—the Declaration of the United States. The Constitution doesn't specifically mention God, but then it doesn't have to because the Declaration is a higher document. The Declaration says that we are a nation under God's laws. Therefore, all other laws of our country should be consistent with the law of God or they violate our national carter.[20]

Figure 1 – THE FOUNDATION OF FREEDOM

CHAPTER THREE

The Plural Minority

THE EROSION OF FREEDOM

The foundation of the Constitution is based upon "the Laws of Nature and of Nature's God." Once again, this is not just any deity imaginable, but rather the deity that is found within the pages of the New Testament. Therefore, the Founding Fathers never intended that the pursuit of individual interests would undermine the foundation of the Constitution.

Neither was it the founders' intention that a minority's interests would undermine the interests of the majority as they relate to the rights protected by the Constitution. In order for this erosion to happen, the people would have to ignore the intention of our forefathers. This type of thinking would certainly destroy every grand idea and law that our founders conceived. Therefore it has to be asked, "Who would do such a thing?" Only one answer is possible. It would have to be a group of people repulsed by the ideas of our forefathers. As a result, they try to stifle the true record of history. These people delight in butchering centuries of indigenous law. The carnage and confusion they leave in their path can only be seen as treasonous. Therefore those individuals should be noted as traitors and enemies of the state.

Much can be learned simply by sampling some of the ideals of the pillars of our government. George Washington embraced, practiced, and taught that "to the distinguished character of Patriot, it should be our highest Glory to add the more distinguished Character of Christian."[21] When the average high school student is asked whether or not America is a Christian nation, what follows is an awkward hesitation then a resounding, "No." Negligence, rhetoric, propaganda, and maverick court rulings from the highest court in the land have brought us to this point.

These rulings are the result of the U. S. Supreme Court ignoring the Constitution in favor of a few comments, taken out of context, from two of the many founders, namely Thomas Jefferson and James Madison. It would be interesting to listen to what these men would say about the present interpretation of the documents they helped to fashion and held so dear. What might they say of a court that has so much power it can strike down any legislative act with the simple decree that it is unconstitutional? Thomas Jefferson speaks for himself on the subject in a letter he wrote to William Jarvis on September 28, 1820:

> You seem...to consider the judges as the ultimate arbiters of all constitutional questions; a very dangerous doctrine indeed, and one which would place us under the despotism

> of an oligarchy. Our judges are as honest as other men, and not more so...and their power [is] the more dangerous as they are in office for life, and not responsible, as the other functionaries are, to the elective control. The Constitution has erected no such single tribunal.[22]

Jefferson made it very clear that to allow the judiciary so much power would undermine the very purpose of the Constitution and the Declaration before that. The Founding Fathers were attempting to throw off tyranny not create a new one of their own. This leads us to what James Madison had to say about the courts. David Barton, a noted conservative historian, in his book *Original Intent*, writes, "Madison had much to say about judges not becoming lawmakers" and then follows with this historical quotation:

> The preservation of a free Government requires not merely, that the metes and bounds which separate each department of power be invariably maintained; but more especially that neither of them be suffered to overleap the great Barrier which defends the rights of the people. The Rulers who are guilty of such an encroachment, exceed the commission from which they derive their authority, and are Tyrants. The People who submit to it are governed by laws made neither by themselves nor by an authority derived from them, and are slaves.[23]

James Madison understood what we now experience. He made it very clear that if the judiciary is allowed by the people to make new laws or nullify old ones, they have become enslaved. According to the Constitution, it is not the judiciary's responsibility to make or nullify laws. The passing of laws is up to elected representatives. One does not have to search very long before he hears of yet another case before a high court aimed at disintegrating the freedoms guarded under the First Amendment. This misuse of judicial power is a nationwide epidemic. It does not matter if we are talking about a crèche display at the county courthouse in Pittsburgh, Pennsylvania,[24] the removal of the Ten Commandments from a courthouse in Alabama[25] or the removal of the cross from a city seal in California.[26]

Why is this happening? Many of the justices in our current and former high courts refuse to consider the full counsel of our history within its proper context. That is exactly what happened in the 1947 court case, *Everson v Board of Education*. This was the first case in which the Supreme Court ruled that religion should be separated from public institutions. The justices based their ruling on a letter that Thomas Jefferson wrote on January 1, 1802, to a group of Baptists that resided in Danbury, Connecticut. They had written the President because of a rumor they heard that the nation was considering the adoption of a single Christian denomination. In order to calm their fears, President Jefferson responded by saying,

> I contemplate with solemn reverence that act of the whole American People which declared that their legislature should "make no law respecting an establishment of religion, or prohibiting the free exercise thereof," thus building a wall of separation between Church and State.[27]

This phraseology did not even originate with Thomas Jefferson but rather with one of the Baptist ministers by the name of Roger Williams. His coining of this phrase was within the context of "the garden of the church and the wilderness of the world." David Barton in his book *The Myth of Separation* quotes John Eidsmoe: "According to Williams, the 'wall of separation' was to protect the 'garden of the church' from the 'wilderness of the world.'"[28] It was not to protect the state from the church. Therefore, to use the statement "the separation of church and state" in order to eradicate Christianity from public institutions is ludicrous. Unfortunately the very fears that Jefferson was trying to calm in the Danbury Baptists have now come true for contemporary Christians. Only in our case, the adopted denomination has become anti-denominationalism, commonly referred to as secularism but more correctly identified as atheism.

This case set a precedent in our country for a barrage of rulings that would follow. Probably the most famous case, at least in the minds of Christians in this country, is the one that ejected prayer from our public schools in 1962, *Engel v Vitale*. This single case overturned centuries of educational practices in America. Up until this case, public schools not only prayed to the God of the Bible but also read about the God of the Bible in both the Old and New Testaments.

Not only did the Supreme Court in this case overturn centuries of American tradition that had been guarded and even upheld by common law, but they did so without citing one previous court case, a new precedent in and of itself. No court in the history of our country had ever before considered making a ruling without referencing multiple precedents. According to Constitutional Historian David Barton,

> Court decisions always cite previous cases as precedents; citing precedent is the means by which the past is used to give

> credibility to the present; precedent serves as the foundation upon which current decisions are built. A significant legal note to this case is that ***not one single precedent was cited by the Court in its removal of school prayer!*** That the Court was able to overturn 340 years of educational history in America without citing a single precedent was an accomplishment of which it was proud, as evidenced by a comment made the following year in the *Abington v. Schempp* case: Finally, in *Engel v. Vitale*, only last year [1962], these principles were so universally recognized that the Court, ***without the citation of a single case*** ... reaffirmed them.[29]

This should seem outrageous to all freedom-loving Americans, especially those who consider themselves true patriots. The last four decades have shown that all someone has to do in any district or town in America today where religious symbols or acts are publicly displayed, is to cry out to the higher courts. The higher courts ignore whether or not an entire school district wants to read the Bible during morning announcements or pray before class. If one student or one parent has a problem with such a practice, then they, with the help of a highly funded legal organization, can force the cessation of such a practice.

In most cases a legal firm with a lot of clout and money simply threatens the particular school district with a lawsuit, and without going to court, those opposed to religious practices are able to impose their will upon the schools governed by that district.

We have lost our resolve to stand firm. Our forefathers risked their lives, their honor, and even their wealth in order to stand firm against tyranny. Today there are legal organizations, such as the American Civil Liberties Union (ACLU), that are dedicated to harassing the Christian segment of the population. These lawyers are the true terrorists of freedom within our country today.

The ACLU claims they stand for civil liberties, but these privileges have nothing to do with the liberties won by our Founding Fathers. The American Civil Liberties Union could just as easily stand for the *American Constitutional Lacerationalists Union*. Not only do they shred the Constitution, but they do so on behalf of communism. Tim LaHaye in his book *Mindsiege* states the point well by citing the United States House of Representatives Special Committee to Investigate Communist Activities in the United States. He quotes:

> The American Civil Liberties Union is closely affiliated with the communist movement in the United States, and fully 90 percent of its efforts are on behalf of communists who have come into conflict with the law. It claims to stand for free speech, free press, and free assembly, but it is quite apparent that the main function of the ACLU is to attempt to protect the communists in their advocacy of force and violence to overthrow the Government, replacing the American flag by a red flag and erecting a Soviet Government in place of the republican form of government guaranteed to each State by the Federal Constitution.[30]

It would probably be more appropriate for the ACLU to rename itself the *American Communists Liberties Union* in light of such evidence. The reason that they will never do such a thing is clear—that type of irresponsible and unabashed audacity would blow their covert operation to overthrow our government. On their own website, they claim that they are dedicated to protecting America from the "tyranny of the majority." This seems to imply that what the majority of Americans want must in some way be tyrannical or unconstitutional. This is an odd formula for a government that has its authority granted by the people. This organization should be renamed the *Aristocratic Civil Liberties Union* or the *Atheistic Civil Liberties Union*. All one has to do is review the cases in which this organization is involved, and he can quickly piece together its agenda—not the upholding of the First Amendment but rather the deterioration of what the framers of the Constitution intended.

The ACLU is both well funded and well organized. In fact, not only do they claim to be about the business of protecting America from the "tyranny of the majority," they also boast in a position paper that "they appear before the Supreme Court more than any other organization."[31] This group has done more to change the legal landscape of America than any other organization in history. Indeed, in the landmark case *Engel v Vitale* in 1962, the Supreme Court that ruled school prayer was unconstitutional actually included a founding member of the ACLU by the name of Felix Frankfurter as one of their justices.[32]

Activist judges such as Felix Frankfurter who try to force their agenda upon a freedom-loving people do not truly understand freedom. In fact, their understanding is tainted. These activist judges cater to a very small group of people at the expense of the majority of our nation's citizens, acting of their own volition, with no regard for the intention of our founding documents. Of course, this is not a recent phenomenon. As was pointed out earlier, both Jefferson and Madison warned of such judicial despotism. Abraham Lincoln even faced judges in his time that were terrors of the law! He had great respect for the Supreme Court throughout the majority of his life, but he had even greater respect for the Constitution and the Declaration of the United States. Therefore, during the Dred Scot case, when the Supreme Court ruled that a slave was not a person but rather property, Lincoln exploded with contempt for the decision. In response to this blatant disregard of the Declaration's statement that "all men are created equal," he declared,

> In order to make slavery eternal and universal, the Declaration is assailed, and sneered at, and construed, and hawked at, and torn, till, if its framers could rise from their graves, they could not at all recognize it.[33]

Lincoln no doubt would be outraged at the high court's blatant disregard for the founders' convictions over the last six decades. In fact, if Abraham Lincoln and the framers he mentioned were alive today, they would not only say this about the Supreme Court's practices concerning the Constitution, but they would also level the same accusation against the practices of the ACLU.

Since there are organizations such as the ACLU that claim on their website "freedom is why we are here," when clearly there are many others who claim that the ACLU has worked against freedom, then we must continue to ask the question, "What is freedom?" But first we have to ask if the definition of freedom, or any word, is attainable. The way a person answers that question reveals his view of the truth.

Figure 2 - REMEMBER THE PAST

THE SECOND LAW OF LIBERTY

DISCOVER THE TRUTH

CHAPTER FOUR

The Tyranny of Truth

THE KNOWLEDGE OF KNOWLEDGE

In order to achieve the knowledge of anything, we have to ask the old philosophical question, "Can anything truly be known?" If nothing can be known, then we, of all countries, are fools for we spend billions of dollars each year educating people in various areas of life. Furthermore, if nothing can be known, sustaining life becomes impossible, for we cannot know whether currency can be exchanged for goods and services such as food; therefore, we must all starve. We also would not know when we were hungry or that we needed food for energy or what type of food to eat. Of course, this line of thinking is absurd because an individual could not know that he could not know whether or not he knew something if he could not truly know anything.

In addition, this kind of reasoning is not practical. Besides the problem of starvation noted earlier, doctors would not be able to diagnose or treat anyone; therefore, in the realm of physical health, we could not know what was wrong with someone who is ill since no standard of health could be known by which to judge or measure a person's well-being.

The attempt to express the fallacies of this position further demonstrates its absurdity, thrusting a thinking individual into an eternity of questions. "What is eternity?" "What are questions?" "How am I reading this book?" "What is reading?" "Am I really reading?" Questioning knowingness or the ability to know anything only leads to stupidity, ignorance, and meaninglessness/confusion.

How then can one know? In order to determine whether the past can be known or not, we have to ask the oldest and most popular question of all philosophical quagmires—"What is true?" This is the most important question for the discussion of freedom. If one cannot discover and practice those things that are true, then one will never truly be free. This concept is at the very core of freedom. Therefore, if truth does not exist, neither does freedom.

Something as basic as communication recognizes the necessity of agreed upon knowledge from the past. Words are symbols by which basic communication takes place. Practically speaking, in order to exist with other communicators we must agree upon our knowledge base. If not, then parents would not be able to give instructions to their children and expect them to be carried out. The work place would become a disaster, unfit for productive activity. Schools would become meaningless. Governments would dissolve. People would become desperate. And survival would become god.[34]

At the very least, in a society where nothing can be known, the basic human instinct of self-preservation would reign supreme and people would, for a short period of time, remain unanswerable to any higher authority. That circumstance would exist as long as it takes a society to submit to someone who knows something about maintaining an environment conducive to survival. Unfortunately, after a time of self-preservation in a chaotic society, people will usually submit to anybody who will save them. History records how entire societies become convinced it is better to submit to the authority of a madman who feeds them than to starve. Therefore, in order to prevent this type of desperate situation, we need to examine the responsibility of truth—*the second law of liberty*.

THE SECOND LAW OF LIBERTY IS TO DISCOVER THE TRUTH

Humans Have Been Designed as Explorers

Knowledge and truth are interdependent. To prove this, we must examine a person's capacity to learn something that is false. He can learn something that is false without knowing the truth, but he cannot understand that it is false unless he knows what is true. Therefore, the goal of knowledge has to be the pursuit of truth. Conversely, the truth can only be known if there is such a thing as knowledge. Yet the goal of knowledge must be truth. Hence the two are interdependent: If that which can be known depends on that which is true, then that which is true can be known.

Consequently, we have to search for and discover the exclusive meaning of truth. The very nature of human existence reveals this quest. By observing a baby, one can see that she not only hungers for a bottle or for food but she also hungers for knowledge. A one-year-old will explore every cupboard in the kitchen. However, children are not satisfied with one expedition. Toddlers can pull everything out of a kitchen drawer today, only to explore the same drawer tomorrow and the next day.

This example illustrates our hunger for knowledge. Because of the interdependence of knowledge with truth, we can surmise that children are also searching for truth.

Children definitely come programmed with this unquenchable desire to learn, but they have to be guided, and even restricted in some cases, simply because their curiosity can lead them into danger. A child does not understand that there are things that can hurt her. Therefore, we adults place covers over certain receptacles in our homes so that the insatiable desire to taste everything will not end up giving her a dangerous jolt.

THE DEFINITION OF TRUTH

Why is it important to know the definition of truth? Because there are many people in our society who believe there are no absolute truths. They will make statements such as, "There are no absolute truths," or "The truth is that there is no truth." These statements are odd since that line of reasoning is self-refuting. For an individual to state that there are no absolute truths, he is depending upon the precedent of truth and the ability to know it in order to draw his conclusion—absurd though it is.

To say that there are no absolute truths, one would have to deduce that absolute statements could not be made. By using the standard and accepted form of an argument (syllogism), we can see the futility in the statement, "There are no absolute truths." Here is the model that we will follow: If absolute statements can be made, then absolute truth exists. Absolute statements can be made. Therefore, absolute truths exist.

What, then, is truth? Many people in our society adhere to different levels and definitions of truth. This variance is revealed in the way they use the word during conversation. Certainly, one acceptable and agreed upon definition would be from the dictionary. Merriam Webster's Collegiate Dictionary states that truth is "fidelity to an original or standard."[35] This concept implies that in order to know the truth about anything, one must know something about the standard by which it is judged to be true or know something about the original.

If the definition of truth means remaining faithful to a standard, then the many people claiming there are no absolute truths must believe there is no standard. If it could be proven that there are absolute truths, what does that require of those who claim there are none? To begin with, it would require they recognize a standard and conform to it. What standard? Whatever the ultimate standard is, whether individuals have acquired the self-realization of it or not. It would have to be the standard from which all truth is derived. We will call this standard God. If there is absolute truth, it must not only be reliable but also identifiable. Furthermore, it must have endured the test of time.

Truth is much like a fully inflated beach ball that a child tries to hold under the surface of water. The ball continues to surface regardless of the child's efforts. The reason for this is that the laws of buoyancy, inertia, and motion are submissive to a standard, and that standard is truth. In the same way, truth continues to surface throughout history.

Just as there are physical laws derived from truth, there must also be ethical laws that stem from the same truth. The moral choices we make have physical consequences. For instance, one is more likely to acquire a sexually transmitted disease if he is promiscuous than if he is not. Most people would agree that lesions or warts on their genitalia are indeed bad things. Yet these "bad things" stem from a physical choice—the consequence of truth. HIV is another truth that many have to live with; this truth is very painful because, at present, there is no cure for the millions who have acquired this disease.

THE ABSOLUTENESS OF TRUTH

"Truth is by its very nature intolerant, exclusive, for every truth is the denial of its opposing error." (Christoph Ernst Luthardt)[36]

A person at this point might agree with the existence of true physical laws but disagree with the fact that there are moral laws that govern the universe. We currently live in a global society that places an equal value upon all worldviews. Many universities encourage their students to respect others' beliefs as their own. However, if truth exists, this is impossible.

Someone might disagree, arguing that all worldviews can be valued equally if one would just open his mind.

Many people have been accused of being close-minded because they adhere to what seems to be a rigid set of moral standards. They may even try to convince others to follow that same set of values. Curiously, those who accuse them of being close-minded are guilty of the same type of close-mindedness. What exactly does *close-minded* mean? One way in which this question can be answered is by referring to an example in the physical realm. Most people will not knowingly ingest glass, harmful drugs, cyanide, snake venom, large quantities of hard liquor, or E. coli because they realize these items would be detrimental to their health. These individuals could not only be accused of being close-minded regarding these substances but also close-bodied. That certainly would not be viewed as a bad thing.

So how does being close-bodied relate to being close-minded? The answer is simple. People close their minds to many areas considered immoral. For instance, most eight-year-old daughters do not have sexual relations with their thirty-six-year-old fathers. This kind of union is not only sick and disgusting but immoral, illegal, and incestuous. If the laws of this government or any government changed to legitimize such perversion, the act would still be immoral because truth exists.

Moreover, if a person believed that his body was powered by a hamster running on a wheel inside him, that belief does not merit the same respect as what we know to be true. Or does the truth depend upon the audience? If the hamster theory was suggested to a two-year-old, he would naively accept the idea.

But if the concept was postulated to an intelligent twelve-year-old, it would be shrugged off as ridiculous—as it should be.

Someone may say, "What is the harm in telling someone that you have a hamster generating power inside your body? If you want to believe that, is that not your prerogative? Besides your belief isn't hurting anyone." Compare this line of thinking with what a parent may teach his child about an old jolly fellow who delivers toys in a red suit on Christmas Eve. This make-believe should never be equated with what we know to be true. It is just something that we share with our children to appeal to their imagination and create a more festive environment around the holidays.

Opening up one's mind is a good thing as long as he is opening it up to the truth and closing it to what is false. If a person opens up his mind to risqué behavior, then he will eventually have to face the filthy consequences of that behavior. Everyone holds to some type of belief system. To what does a person's belief system expose him? Do we really want to afford the same value to all systems of belief when some are obviously more susceptible to malignant behavior than others? We should not, if truth exists.

If we try to maintain that all systems of belief are truly equal, what happens if a person believes that ingesting cyanide is actually healthy for the body? One could only hope that a civilized society would squelch such nonsense. Taking it one step further, what happens to this argument when placed in a society that claims it values education? One might argue that education protects a society from nonsense. A person from some primitive, stone-age society, for instance, would be more apt to believe a story about the healthy properties of cyanide. Granted, education protects a society from nonsense, but can it protect society from nonsense if the educational system has lapsed into nonsense? Can an educational system be beneficial if it purports that all value systems are equally true? If truth cannot be ascertained, then the answer is yes! If the truth can be established, then the answer is absolutely not! If there is such a thing as truth, then all belief systems are not equal; therefore, not all value systems should be granted the same merit or time in the classroom.

In a society that values education apart from the truth, it is possible not only to have individuals promoting false information in the realm of health but it is also possible for them to do so legitimately. This can be illustrated by returning to the example of a person who believes that ingesting cyanide into the body is healthy. What happens if this person went through an educational system that taught that truth is what you make it; that there may be things true for one group of people but not true for another? So this person goes through school and eventually graduates as a bona fide nutritionist with the credentials. A society that values education but tries to maintain that all beliefs are universally equal would produce a cyanide-wielding nutritionist who says that it is his firm belief that cyanide is healthy for the body and that he is offended by anyone who repudiates his belief. Is this the type of belief that a society wants to promote? Is this person's belief equal to that of a nutritionist who earnestly studies the historical and scientific data in order to make proven statements about what affects the body's longevity? It would be ridiculous to claim that both opposing views are equally valuable.

But who cares if a nutritionist believes cyanide is good for the body? If he believes that to the point of putting it into practice, he eventually ingests and rids the world of himself. What is the harm in that? One of the dangers that could develop is that others may follow in his footsteps. Worse yet, what if this self-enlightened nutrition guru begins to teach others that cyanide is the way to achieving the ultimate physical peace or the final experience?[37] Then we could end up with another Jim Jones and the Guyana affair.[38]

What is the point of such absurdity? Since everyone believes something, the focus of our society should not be placed upon the value of a person's belief or even on how much an individual treasures his belief. We as a society should not be pressured or manipulated into accepting all beliefs as equal, nor should the focus be placed upon individual belief.

Some children have believed that everyone around them was a robot, and they were the only real human beings. Still other children may relate people they see to other people they already know. For instance, a child who does not see an aunt or an uncle for a long period of time may associate that relative with a famous movie star based upon superficial similarities between the relative and the star. Children have fantastical ideas, and we should expect such things from them. But when we claim that all ideas should be held with equal esteem so as not to offend anybody, we are, essentially, reducing the intellect of our society as a whole. We are asked to embrace belief systems that are juvenile and spurious, not to mention dangerous.

This should bring a thinking person to understand that the question is not whether or not he believes something, for everyone believes something, but rather whether or not his belief is true. This demands a society to analyze a given belief in the area of its foundation. This analytical formula seeks to answer the question, "What is this belief founded upon?" If the belief is founded upon error, then it can be dismissed. This is the way a thinking society can keep itself free from deceptive ideas. No one should be forced to hold an erroneous belief to be true. Not only do erroneous beliefs dumb down a society, but more importantly, they erode the freedom that we value dearly.

WHEN TRUTH IS CONSIDERED TRUE

The Attack of the Clones

So when should truth be considered truth? A line from the movie *Star Wars: Episode 2* may help us better understand the importance of answering such a question. The scene depicts a librarian along with a character named Obi-Wan Kenobi. In this scene, Obi-Wan is struggling to find a planet that some old-timer told him about. However, when he enters that sector shown on his computer's map, the planet does not appear. He then beckons for the assistance of the librarian, and she responds, "If an item does not appear in our records, it does not exist." Later in the movie, it is revealed that the planet existed all along. It was merely deleted from the official record for a time by another individual who wanted to keep it hidden.[39] This one scene can illustrate an epidemic within our society today, namely, that if something has not been discovered or if it has been discovered and then hidden or revised by a contemporary academician, many believe it does not exist.

Crud vs. Creature

There are individuals in the intellectual community today who persuade modern educational institutions to embrace certain ideas while shunning others that may actually have more factual and supportive evidence. For instance, for the majority of our nations' history we embraced the model of creation as recorded in the Hebrew Scriptures, but today most educational institutions in the United States are pressured to hold to the modern enlightened view of evolution as the explanation for the origins of everything. Actually the idea is not that modern. In fact, the concept was rejected by most scholars throughout recorded history.[40] But today an uphill rhetorical battle is ahead for the few institutions that choose to baulk at the coercion to teach the evolutionary model. This rhetoric usually comes in the form of labels leveled against these more traditional institutions. They are accused of being primitive, unlearned, and antiquated, not to mention religious and intolerant.

What does this squabble have to do with truth or even the American idea of freedom? Is this not just another fight right wing extremists are picking with science? Absolutely not! Both creation and evolution are just theories—that is, unless one can be proven true. Since none of us existed at the time of our planet's inception, what if we can never prove conclusively one or the other to be true? At this point, it would seem that we should adhere to the model that has produced the most tangible evidence. Evolutionary proponents are eager to point out that in their opinion, the creation account as it is recorded in the Book of Genesis is nothing more than a Jewish myth. Creation Scientists argue that evolution is just a theory. Why go on and on about such a matter? Because we have regressed in the area of knowing when truth is considered truth.

Remember, the difference between whether someone believes something and what they believe in are two different issues. The value is not placed upon the fact that he believes. (One is not noble simply because he holds to some sort of system). The emphasis needs to be placed upon what a person believes. By determining the factual value of the object of belief, then and only then, can we determine how valuable the belief is. The object of faith is more important than faith itself. One's belief in something does not create the object of his belief, if indeed his belief is based in fact. Belief should stem from fact; fact does not stem from belief. We can believe that something exists, search for it, and discover it, but it always existed whether or not we discovered, searched, or believed. Its discovery may have been determined by our belief; however, its existence was not. Faith derives its life from fact. For if a person's faith is not based in fact, it is fiction. Therefore, factual evidence should be ascertained to establish faith.

The goal of those who love freedom should be to encourage others to throw off error and embrace truth. Whether a person believes something does not matter as much as what he believes. Belief for the sake of belief is futile. Belief must be grounded in truth. Is truth considered truth because a human being with some credentials proposes a theory? Or are we willing to objectively expose these theories to the scrutiny of honest individuals who want to know which is true? Who cares if the creation account is recorded in the Book of Law of the Jewish people? If Moses was correct in recording what was passed down to him as that which happened "in the beginning…," should that not be embraced?

The argument of origins is a core element in ultimate knowledge. The argument is a hostile battle that rages within a much deeper war. The war in the abstract is over whether or not a Supreme Creator truly does exist. Although the sides may be distorted at times, when polarized they are distinct—monotheists on one side and atheists on the other. Humans have to decide whether or not they are willing to succumb to the assumptions of atheists or the tradition of monotheists.

This is when it becomes more important to focus upon what we believe rather than whether we believe. The focus has to be centered upon facts, not preference. The first fact that Mankind must deal with is that there is *something* here. The fact that there is something here as opposed to nothing, to most people is evidence that there is someone, somewhere who thought of something. Thinking individuals must not regard themselves to be so esoteric as to proclaim that the creation account is just religiosity with its certified biases. If creation is dismissed because of its connection to religion, then public educators need to rethink their position on teaching evolution in the modern schoolroom because the US Supreme Court has labeled atheism a religion as do most universities today.[41] Most thinking individuals understand that

Darwinian evolution is the "Genesis 1:1" of atheists. Labeling something as religious does not automatically disqualify it from being factual.

What standard of truth is being used to disqualify a document simply because it has been categorized as religious? Are we using accurate science by claiming that a document cannot be true if it has a religious origin? Should a society think itself more intelligent because it boasts that none of its loftiest ideas originated from religious thought or documentation? Certainly our society cannot boast of such nonsense. As has been demonstrated already, even a shallow perusal of comments from our Founding Fathers reveals that their ideas for common law come directly from the religion of Christianity.

A thinking person can conclude that, society must cultivate an environment that provides the greatest number of people with the greatest number of opportunities to discover truth. If that means allowing creation back into the classroom in an attempt to wrestle with and answer the true origin of human existence, then so be it. One cannot simply write off another person's belief system until that system of thinking has been proven untrue. If that has not happened, then we, as a society, should be more open to the system, especially if there are qualitative facts pointing us in that direction. Obviously, we have to be cautious not to delve into absurdities. But in the realm of meaningful and practical truth, we should be allowed to pursue passionately the strictest model possible. Like a sculptor working on a masterpiece, we need to have the liberty to chisel away falsities so that we can achieve an image as close to the original as possible. This pursuit should not be stifled by labels.

Insolence vs. Intolerance

One label that is used to win many arguments in the debate over truth today is the idea of *tolerance*. Many people throw this word around without thinking their logic through. Take, for instance, the expression of vulgarity that is so prevalent within our society.[42] A person who values propriety may tolerate a friend who is using profanity in front of him. If he feels compelled to tell him to watch his language, the friend might respond, "You just need to be a little more tolerant of other people's language." The prudent individual could respond by saying, "Since your view of tolerance is intolerant of my view of tolerance, let's tolerate the intolerance of our tolerance some other time." This example demonstrates that the word *tolerance* can be thrown into any conversation in an attempt to stifle another person. The only problem with this meaning of tolerance is that one can have it immediately turned against him in the same way.

The cry for tolerance does not defeat a position grounded in truth. Conversely, it shows how weak or lazy the person's position is since he has failed to build an argument. If our argument for truth is going to be based upon facts rather than labels and rhetoric, what are some facts concerning Man's origin? Can we, by observing the outcome of two competing theories, determine which one holds more weight? This approach is necessary in the debate over origins because we were not there. Consequently, we have to consider the premises of each model and then observe the results of the presuppositions. This approach is not a biological argument but rather a philosophical one based upon factual outcomes.

Evolution claims that humans have evolved from beasts; the biblical account of creation claims that humans have been created in the image of God. Genesis 1:27 states, "So God created people in his own image; God patterned them after himself; male and female he created them."

There is a fundamental difference between these two positions. One says that we have evolved from the image of a beast; the other states that we were created by and in the image of an Almighty God. One model claims that we have come from something lower than ourselves and, therefore, are now higher. The other model claims that we have come from something higher than ourselves. Evolutionists present what they believe to be a high view of humanity. Their model limits humanity by the finiteness of a closed universe. The creation model, on the other hand, liberates humanity by the infinite creativity of an Almighty God and actually places the human within the very image of the highest position possible, namely God.

CHAPTER FIVE

The Piracy of Love

CUPID OR STUPID

If we, as a society, adhere to evolution, then what obligation do people have to love one another? Can an atheist who claims chance, accident, and chaos as his model of origin truly love his neighbor as himself? Can he love at all and still maintain his worldview?[43] Certainly there are atheists who love and care for their own children, but are they being consistent with their worldview? Their worldview states that there is no Supreme Being from which a standard of love can be derived. Therefore, love must be contrived by the individual atheist and his surrounding environment. An atheist simply adheres to the position that love is something that a society determines. It is up to the society to define it; it is up to the society to design it; it is up to the society to refine it. But history has proven time and time again that all a society can do to love is malign it.

Abuses are obvious in societies that allow their definition of love to be determined by consensus. One does not have to search very long in order to find some examples. Whether we observe the Nazi atrocities at Auschwitz, the American example of slavery, or the sentencing of an innocent Jew to death by crucifixion, all of these can be held up as classic examples of abuse, the antithesis of loving one's neighbor. That is what happens when love is simply allowed to fall to the hands of an individual or to the consensus of society.

Love is the system of measurement that assesses the freedom of humanity. How then, can humanity measure itself?[44] If while exercising you notice a stamp of forty-five pounds on an iron cast weight that you have been using to shape your muscles, you may accept that it is forty-five pounds, or you might weigh it. Someone may argue that one could weigh it against another plate of the same value, but what would determine the weight of the comparison plate? In the realm of ideas, therein lies a fundamental difference between atheism and theism—a theist, one who believes there is a God, recognizes that a scale is needed. Not just any scale, but a scale that is tested, calibrated, and able to handle the weight of that which is being weighed.

Theists who believe God created not only the physical universe apart from any accident or gap in time, understand that love is measured by the Almighty Scale that towers above humanity. Humans are measured against God's standard of love because love is a manifested attribute of the deity. However, just as a weight cannot be used to measure a weight of the same mass apart from the use of a scale, love cannot be measured by the Almighty Scale unless the scale had a way of both measuring love and *being* Love at the same time.

THE RECIPROCATING ENGINE OF LOVE

Enter Christianity. Christianity promotes the idea of monotheism in trinity. This idea was not contrived but was actually revealed by Jesus Christ. The purpose was that Love, the Father, sent Love, the Son or the True Image of Love, to be measured or translated by Love, the Holy Spirit. The Holy Spirit is the scale; Jesus Christ (God incarnate) is set upon the scale against anyone who claims to love, and the Father judges the results. Christians believe that love is measured against the true example of love, Jesus Christ. He is not only the one who revealed that there is no greater love than this that a man would lay down his life for his friends,[45] but also is the one who demonstrated that we should love our enemies.[46]

THE PIRACY OF LOVE

Conversely, atheism on its own cannot make such claims. Atheism can borrow these lofty ideas from Christ, but in doing so, it violates its own position, rendering the atheist inconsistent with his worldview. Why? Because love, by its very nature, is reciprocal. The reciprocal nature of love requires that it must be directed toward something or someone. Atheism cannot produce love because it fails to recognize that love originates somewhere outside of humanity. Certainly humans can demonstrate love, but demonstration is only possible because they have observed fellow humans demonstrating love. Since atheists assert that there is no God, they must derive their understanding of love solely from tradition, social conditioning, and genetic formation. However, this will quickly prove to be an inadequate reference for love because it is too limited in scope. Society must base its morality upon something outside of and higher than itself; otherwise it becomes ethnocentric and releases people to feel as though they can legitimately exhibit contemptuous behavior toward others.

Therefore, these questions must be posed to an atheist: "What would you do if there was no society or previous genetic information that demonstrated love? What if you were the first man?" According to the atheist's view, there would be no source outside humanity to gauge or determine what love is. Furthermore, since you would be the first man, there would be no previous genetic information from *Homo sapiens* to reflect upon. Therefore, a strict interpretation of atheism would require you to believe you only have the paternal, genetic information passed to you from the beast from which you came.

The genetic information from a monkey or an ape does not satisfy the question where love comes from. The beast can grunt, copulate, and care for its young, but it cannot formulate the higher expressions of love that mankind can. For instance, a man can be moved by compassion to help out an injured animal, whatever the species. But have you seen what a lioness does to an injured gazelle? Never in the history of the pride has a lioness ministered first aid to a gazelle. Have you ever seen a cat minister to an injured mouse? It does not happen, but a human could nurse a mouse back to health, if he so desired. Has there ever been a turkey buzzard that has helped a deer clipped by an automobile and suffering? The answer is, "No." The buzzards circle above the animal and poke at it every once in a while until they are satisfied that it will not resist consumption. A human, however, could attempt to save the life of the deer. Furthermore, a man can save the life of his enemy because men have been given the capacity to minister to their enemies. Geneticists have taught us that an organism's genetic makeup will never produce anything outside of itself except the information that is present within the organism. Organisms can lose genetic information, but they can never gain new information.[47] Although love is above and beyond some genetic organization of cells, it abides most completely within the species that we refer to as human.

Since our lone atheist is the first man, he has no society to reflect upon, and since his genetic information is not going to assist him in his understanding of love, how in the world will he learn about love to pass on to the next mutated clone of the slough? He will not be able to do so because there would be no one else from whom to display or reciprocate love. We have not even examined the necessity of the timing of mutual evolution.

Mutual evolution simply means that beyond the probability of infinitesimal chain reactions, we have to end up with the evolution of two humans simultaneously, or within the same lifespan, in order for there to be the possibility of a demonstration of love. This idea, in and of itself, is absurd.

At the time of the first evolved man's self-realization he would be completely alone. How would he discover love amidst other organisms still in the mutated slime of transition? Even if there was another human somewhere on the earth who had made the transition to *Homo sapiens,* he would still have to find that other human. Even if the two found each other, which is highly unlikely on this huge planet, how would they demonstrate an act of love they have never observed? Furthermore, how do we know that their "survival instinct" would not kick in? They might try to kill one another, the antithesis of love.

This scenario is exactly what evolution purports must happen. One might object at this point that this first human could possibly observe other animals that are present. From animals, he might learn how they care for their own, but are they going to care for him the way they care for their young, or are they going to run? This is a vicious cycle that continually forces one back to the original question: where did love come from?

I LOVE; THEREFORE, I AM

Another person might object that the first human could have come to a realization of self-love. This is an interesting objection because we realize that even toddlers who have descended from a long genetic line of humans have to be taught self-realization. They have to be taught where their nose, eyes, and mouth are because they cannot see them. They do, however, have some self-realization, but even that is without complete understanding. Most people have seen an infant watch with a sense of wonder as he observes his hand move. But in order for self-love to be realized, love has to be observed and love for the self must be available.

Someone might interject that feeding oneself is a form of love. That is untrue; eating is just another element of self-preservation, much like breathing. The reason that eating cannot be used as an argument for self-love is that the first evolved human would not know why his belly growls. This rings true even for humans today. Babies cry, but the adults who have experienced hunger and thirst in the past are the ones who diagnose a crying baby and provide food. Therefore, the adult who provides food for the helpless baby is demonstrating love. Babies have to be taught what to eat, even in this enlightened age. One would think that if evolution were true, certainly by now, a child should know not to place mud, rocks, sticks, bugs, bird feces, or previously chewed gum that is sticking to the sidewalk in his mouth. But one of the many facts that every parent realizes is that children have to be taught not to stick foreign objects in their mouths. In other words, there has to be a revelation of self-preservation. Self-preservation has to be taught; it has to be revealed. So where does love come from? A strict atheist would have to conclude that love does not exist and that everything is done out of self-preservation or selfishness.

The atheistic position is untenable because of the fact that it fails to recognize in its purest state the reciprocation of self-realization. In order to know something outside of the self, there has to be something outside of the self to know. Reality is reciprocal. If there is nothing outside of the self that can be known, then nothing can be known, which means truth and love, both of which are two very necessary components of freedom, become non-existent. If there is something outside the self, then truth and love do exist and at least one other being that is greater than the self must have acted.

THE DNA OF LOVE AND HATE

We have now come to a point where the fundamental flaw of evolution can be exposed. In any argument, one must be cautious not to build his entire argument upon assumptions. The primary assumption in the evolutionary model is intelligence. An evolutionist will go on and on about how wonderful it is that such and such a species has the ability to develop biologically whatever it will need for survival. What is the source of this intelligence? Intelligence is the primary constitution of humanity. Where did it come from? Evolutionists make continual references to advancements and developments that have taken place over the last six hundred million years, but what they are really making reference to is "assumed intelligence."

Intelligence has to come from somewhere. In order to gain intelligence, a person has to be exposed to more intelligence or someone who is more intelligent. Therefore, the creationist recognizes that in order for there to be intelligence, intelligence had to be. If intelligence is the originator of intelligence, then there must be a Creator who is intelligent. This is the point where an evolutionist finds himself entangled in a web of truth. He can either admit that there is indeed an intelligent creator, or he can attempt to avoid the subject.

Another flaw that stems from assumed intelligence is the idea of survival of the fittest. In order for a species to know that it needs to survive, it has to be intelligent enough to know that its existence is threatened. Evolutionists assume that the fear of extinction is so great that the desire for survival will be greater. What is interesting is that even though the intelligent species has a desire for survival and a fear of extinction, extinction still looms over every species in existence. Not one of them has conquered extinction.

We could call this second flaw, "assumed survival." Not only does a species have to have the intelligence to know it needs to survive, but it also has to recognize its need for survival. Furthermore, a species has to have the means necessary to defend itself when its survival is threatened. Without eyes, ears, nose, mouth, hands, fists, legs, feet, heart, lungs, stomach, brain, cardiovascular, nervous and digestive systems already in place, survival is impossible for a creature simply because a species does not have time (another thing that is very much assumed by evolutionists) to develop claws, teeth, legs, arms, or wings while living in a threatening environment.[48]

Why the need for survival anyway? How would a creationist respond to this very question? By studying the biblical record in Genesis 3, one can find out a perfectly logical explanation. If there is an intelligent creator, then it would follow that His creation would indeed be subject to His knowledge. To ignore His knowledge would be to subject oneself to ignorance, not to mention that it would be detrimental to one's own survival. The fact that we, as humans, have the option of choosing to follow His knowledge is a demonstration of our capacity for working together in a coordinated effort of cooperation with the Creator. This is the essence of knowledge.[49]

Knowledge grants creation, specifically humans, the opportunity to become co-creators with the Creator; the result is friendship. The fact that we can read, write, speak, and interact rationally demonstrates the ability to make calculated choices. This ability to make choices grants us the opportunity to exercise our freedom. Within the realm of freedom then, we ultimately have two choices—dependence upon self, which leads to certain doom and destruction, or dependence upon the Creator, which activates life and industry. If by the law of design we are intrinsically dependent upon the Creator, then we should recognize that our most direct route to freedom and survival is to recognize this dependency and make choices that demonstrate our understanding.

One of the greatest joys a father has is when his child realizes that in order to solve a given problem, he sometimes has to humble himself and turn to his father and depend upon him for help. Likewise, when a child is injured or his feelings are wounded, a mother takes delight that her child looks to her in order to make everything better. The child, in both instances, has the ability to look elsewhere for help, but he realizes that his fastest track to relief is going to be found in the one who procreated or adopted him.

Admittedly, the goal of childrearing is to develop an independent adult. But even though a child may be trained to conduct himself independently and in a civil manner, he is never to work against his parents so as to harm them because he thinks he no longer needs them or their knowledge. He is expected to work together in a coordinated effort assisting the family to grow stronger than it was before. This is the camaraderie of cooperation and the very essence of love. If a child was to do something that would harm the rest of the family, the child would have to be disciplined and maybe even isolated until he could be brought back into cooperation successfully. If the child, as an adult, is defiantly bent against the efforts of the family to the detriment of the others or the unit, eventually he would have to be cut off.

Families are a major impetus for truth and love. Humans exist to relate. In order to relate, we have to cooperate. In order to cooperate, we have to communicate. The more honest and exhaustive the communication is, the better the relationship will be. Therefore, from a relational perspective, truth and love have always existed. Truth therefore, is the external eternal that makes it possible to love the internal provisional. Truth and love are very personal. These personal qualities of truth and love act as the mortar that binds the mortal to the immortal.

The truth does not become truth; it is discovered or revealed. Whether or not an individual recognizes the truth does not change the reality of its existence. Universal truth cannot be changed. An individual may refuse to recognize it out of stubbornness or ignorance, but that does not change the reality of truth. In fact, the individual who ignores the truth will have the personal consequences of truth persuading him to embrace the truth.

God only knows how many consequences we have faced as a nation because we have ignored the revelation of truth and have developed our own modes of love instead. Violent crimes alone have increased at an unprecedented rate over the last five decades.[50] Sexually transmitted diseases have increased to the point that one in four Americans now has an STD.[51] The Center for Disease Control and Prevention Department of Health and Human Services reported in January 2004 that "It has been estimated that at least 50% of sexually active men and women acquire genital HPV (Human Papillomavirus) infection at some point in their lives."[52] This disease causes genital warts, a condition for which there is no cure.

A very simple solution to this problem is to teach young people not to have sex before marriage, so that they can enter into a marriage covenant someday completely pure and without the need of a cure. The truth is that when two people come together in a monogamous, heterosexual union for life, there need not be any concern over STD's. These diseases could be eliminated in one generation. Unfortunately, such information is not tolerated. Instead, it is pulverized by legal groups, in the name of the First Amendment, who promote the absurd but demote that which is common sense. It seems any solution involving abstinence offered as legitimate, proactive, or preventative is shuffled off because of religious underpinnings or labeled as religious education with the result that few learn the truth and try it. Why does this happen? We have sexual diseases rising at epidemic rates, and we are not allowed to teach abstinence in most public school settings. What is the purpose of education if not to equip a person with the truth so that he can make wise decisions that will promote the well-being of all? Education should not restrict the truth in the name of so-called civil liberties. Common sense should tell us that more liberties will be enjoyed if we examine a teaching and the results of the teaching, then decide whether this teaching is beneficial or detrimental to the masses based upon the facts.

EMBRACE THE TRUTH

The fact is that people, especially young people in our educational institutions, are not being allowed the opportunities to embrace the truth. Special interest groups are more concerned about their own pet behaviors they refer to as civil liberties, than they are for the well-being of our children. These groups claim that restricting sexual training to one model, such as abstinence and monogamous heterosexual unions for life, quenches the spirit of liberty.

Unfortunately, these same groups are quenching the spirit of liberty by neglecting the consequences of truth. Every worthy parent understands this concept. If an eighteen-month-old tries to place her finger inside an electrical outlet, a good parent will shout, "No!" If the child does not understand *no*, she may continue the attempt, but a parent who realizes the danger that lurks behind the wall will intervene. The reason that the good parent will intervene is because he is willing to sacrifice the brief satisfaction that the child will receive from getting her own way for the enduring satisfaction that she will receive from staying away from something that could prove to be lethal. Freedom for the child, in this case, actually comes from parental restrictions. Even though the child's action is restricted, it is through this restriction that allows her freedom to flourish. Many people in our society do not understand this concept. Instead of teaching young people to exercise self-control, they are willing to pay for unbridled passions with the lives of the masses.

CHAPTER SIX

VIRTUE AND VICE AND EVERYTHING NAUGHTY

THE MODERN IDEA OF EQUALITY PLACED UPON BELIEF AND TRUTH

ANOTHER REASON WHY CHILDREN in the educational institutions of America today are having such a difficult time discovering and embracing the truth is that it is obscured. There is a pervasive idea within the educational curriculum not only that all ideas are equal, but that there is also an equality placed upon belief and truth. For instance, the accepted norm is that most teenagers are going to discover sex on their own and experiment. This belief then drives the educational institutions to interfere with sexual development by dedicating an entire curriculum to sex education. We could call this "Experimenting across the Curriculum." Since the educational establishment in America has been convinced that belief equals truth, they teach as equally valid all the different ways that humans can engage in sexual behavior. Sex before marriage now becomes a viable option; homosexuality is looked upon as a legitimate alternate life style. Therefore, our children are saturated with sexual information because the establishment states that they will have sex regardless.

What is even more amazing is that many consider it irresponsible not to teach sex education in schools. However this view contradicts the presupposition. If belief and truth are equal, why should anyone oppose parents taking the responsibility to teach their own children about sex? Furthermore, if belief and truth are equal, then why do our educational institutions ignore the vast number of parents who desire their children to wait until marriage before engaging in sex? "Wait until marriage!" They scoff and discount the idea as barbaric. So our society continues to believe that since children are going to have sex anyway, adults should provide them with as many models as possible without suggesting any are moral or immoral, and should allow them to make their own decisions.

Are the academic elite who make policy teachers or car salesmen? Giving children behavioral options without equipping them with the ability to choose which is wrong and which is right is not teaching. In fact, our society has proven that when this model of teaching is adopted as the norm, that which had been condemned becomes condoned and that which has been condoned becomes condemned. If a person is not teaching morality, then he is not teaching.

If our goal is freedom, then our approach to education must be free, universal, and absolute. We must understand that, though there is no limit to how many people can be free, there is a limit to the degree of freedom people can enjoy. How wrong to teach that all beliefs are equal and then turn around and withhold equal time in the classroom for some beliefs. The fact is, some educators do not allow certain values to be taught in the classroom, not because they are religious values, but rather because they know the truth: all beliefs are not equal. They do not want all beliefs to be viewed as equal, but they also do not want people to know that they do not want all beliefs to be viewed as equal. So they continue to smother the fire of truth with their blanket of obscurity in order to create enough of a smokescreen so they will not be called hypocrites. The fact is that some beliefs are more valuable than others, and right now, public schools teach what they say is more valuable. If they truly wanted all beliefs to be viewed as equal, then they would have to allow equal class time for all views. They would also have to make sure that all views were taught with the same amount of conviction.

Therefore, when it comes to teaching sex education, educators in public institutions condemn no sexual behavior except *no sexual behavior*. The very thing that is condemned is the one in which there is no room for condemnation. We have become a condom nation, in the name of equality. So we sterilize everything, hoping that some things will remain sterilized. There are many areas in life that would not require micro sterilization (prophylactics) if macro sterilization (heterosexual monogamous marriage) was practiced.

Unfortunately, in most of the educational institutions in this country, the truth is suppressed; teenagers are being taught that no matter how irresponsible, they may have sex with whomever, whenever, and however they would like. They are taught that the time to unlock the chastity belt is when they feel it is right. If that time occurs in the back of someone's car or on prom night or at a football game, that is their choice to make. No one can tell them one way or the other what to do, as long a they use a condom. Incidentally, are not the promoters of condom usage telling young people what to do? Once again, within this euphoric model, no consequences will be considered because that would be moral or religious instruction in a public institution. Who in the world decided that moral instruction in the public arena would do harm to the public? It is as if teenage boys have gotten a hold of the curriculum, and they want to brainwash as many girls as they can into giving up their virginity.

Clearly, as a society we have allowed many of the academic elite who drive the educational curriculum to equate, or better yet, substitute, preference for truth. When any group suppresses truth, society must examine history in order to understand the consequences of suppressing truth. Has there ever been a time in the past when educators, scientists, and thinkers ignorantly promoted fiction as fact? Yes. There is a common myth that some of the most celebrated thinkers in the fifteenth century thought the earth was flat. This myth saturated the American landscape in the early eighteenth century and for the last two centuries found a place in many textbooks. The problem with claiming that most fifteenth century thinkers thought the earth was flat is that the statement is untrue. Lee Strobel in his book, *The Case For A Creator,* writes the following:

> David Lindberg, former professor of the history of science and currently director of the Institute for Research in the Humanities at the University of Wisconsin, said in a recent

> interview: One obvious [myth] is that before Columbus, Europeans believed nearly unanimously in a flat Earth—a belief allegedly drawn from certain biblical statements and enforced by the medieval church. This myth seems to have had an eighteenth century origin, elaborated and popularized by Washington Irving, who flagrantly fabricated evidence for it in his four-volume history of Columbus.... The truth is that it's almost impossible to find an educated person after Aristotle who doubts that the Earth is a sphere. In the Middle Ages, you couldn't emerge from any kind of education, cathedral school or university, without being perfectly clear about the Earth's sphericity and even its approximate circumference.[53]

The acceptance of this myth is a prime example of people thinking they were on the cutting edge of truth, while in reality they were crippling it. As a result of this suppression of facts, educators, knowingly or unknowingly, led people to believe that fifteenth century thinkers consistently stalled one of the most important discoveries ever to be made by man.

Someone might argue, students who were falsely taught to believe that people in the fifteenth century thought that the earth was flat, believed what they believed based upon the tradition or history that had been passed down to them. Therefore, we ought to throw out all traditional thought and begin as if we know nothing. This kind of thinking is juvenile. A society should not frivolously throw away the entire history of man's recorded thoughts simply because there were faulty traditions based upon fear or fabrication. On the contrary, a thinking society should go back as far into history as possible, and based upon historic examples and proven principles, determine what is true and what is false.

Educators today who claim that teenagers are going to have sex no matter what are behaving just like the people who based their knowledge of fifteenth century thought upon fictitious eighteenth century information. Contemporary educators are behaving like nineteenth century instigators who taught lies about the early navigators. They claim they are the ones fanning the flames of discovery while advocates of abstinence are extinguishing them. In reality, statistics have shown that the only flames they have fanned are the damaging results of perversion and disease. Our society, by and large, may be the most sexually educated society in the history of mankind. As a result, we have seen a rise in sexual crimes such as adultery, rape, incest, child molestation, and sexual harassment.

Regardless of the evidence demonstrating these consequences, educators in this country continue to teach the catechism of sexuality without morality. This vicious cycle continues until prom night when the uninitiated are encouraged to step into the unchaste world of reckless behavior. The beauty and splendor of the pageantry have been exchanged for the pressures that go along with promiscuity. Unfortunately, in this case, the students become the products of their education. As a result, prom stands for promiscuity. The policy makers of this type of instruction advocate that teens, like the people of the fifteenth century, are flat in their thinking.

How is the "safe-sex" rationale any different from saying that teens are going to smoke marijuana so we must teach them to smoke it safely? What kind of prophylactic can we invent to place over their mouths so they can inhale to their hearts' content? The answer, of course, is that there isn't one, at least not one that will protect them from the negative effects that pot will have upon their minds. Whether a person is inhaling marijuana smoke into his lungs or lasciviousness into his mind, both will have an effect upon his actions, and no latex is going to stop the pandemic effects that this behavior will have upon our society.

VIRTUE AND VICE AND EVERYTHING NAUGHTY

Teenagers are not flat in their thinking. They are not at the mercy of their sexual urges. And the only education that is going to protect this upcoming generation is the truth—progress only comes through order, and order only comes from consistent and controlled behavior. Well-rounded virtue can only be taught through self-control. Virtue certainly does not develop by hooking a person upon a single addiction and then teaching him his involvement was inevitable. Obsession whether natural or manufactured always leads to vice.[54]

There is no doubt that humans, at our core, are creatures of vice. Unfortunately, we become slaves of habits that will eventually kill us. Now within our society we have legislators and educators who stand by as guardians *of* vice.

Some people have argued that sex and marijuana are both natural and ought to be enjoyed. Others have gone so far as to include God in this equation by making statements such as "God created these pleasures so they must be good." Yes, God has created these items; He has also created human hands.

The truth about human hands is that they can be used to strangle or to stroke; to caress or to kill; to crush or to coddle.

This point once again forces us to recognize our obligation to act responsibly. Additionally, we must also recognize that if we are going to draw God into the argument, we would be remiss if we failed to note that after God declared everything He created to be good, man rebelled against Him. Rebellion against God opened up a whole new frontier for mankind to endure.

Prior to the rebellion, the good God could relate perfectly to the good man—the good man had a good relationship with the good God and perfectly understood that God alone defined what was good for man. It was clear to the good man that the good God, by His very nature, was the ultimate good. Since God is the ultimate good, then He alone defines goodness. Since He alone defines goodness, in order for anything to be considered good, it would have to measure up to His divine standard of goodness. Anything that does not measure up to his divine standard of goodness could not be considered good. He alone, being the Creator, holds the sole authority to define that which is good.

This cannot be changed or challenged without contending with the Creator and the meaning of goodness. Therefore, since God is good, He cannot relate to anything that is evil. To think that he could relate to evil would be like a living man attempting to have sexual relations with a dead woman in order to reproduce himself. Even though they both have essentially the same material makeup, the man is living, and the woman is dead. They cannot be equally fulfilled. There will be no warmth, no passion, no reciprocation or response and certainly no conception from the cold, lifeless woman.

In the same way, God cannot relate to evil because evil is the opposite of good. Therefore, if the good man defies the good God, then the man is no longer good but evil. In fact, just one evil act, one deviation, one inconsistent moment from the good man would infinitely separate him from the incessantly good God.

Therefore, after the rebellion, the good God could not relate to the evil man because there was nothing good left within the man to which the good God could relate. God was the force behind the goodness of man; God gave man the freedom to embrace that goodness. However, being the good God that He is, he also gave man the freedom to choose evil. If God had not given man this choice, then man would be a mindless zombie. Man without choice would not be a separate entity from God who was capable of choosing goodness, and therefore, would not be liable for his actions. In order for someone to be considered good or evil, he has to have the capacity for goodness. There has to be a trial or a test of the mind. He can either choose to conform to the established standard or rebel against it.

Man has the capacity to choose good or evil, which, in and of itself, is an argument for a higher standard of morality. Therefore, man apparently was designed with the capability either to submit to good or to subject himself to evil. In order to be held accountable to the standard, man would have to be equipped with a full understanding of what was expected of him by the standard.

Out of all the men that have existed, the first man was qualified for goodness. Not only was he created good, but he also completely understood good without any knowledge of evil. There was no tension in his mind. In fact, the odds of choosing good were stacked in his favor. He was created good; he only knew good and thus was expected to be good and to choose good. However, once man fell, he did not have the power to retrieve God's goodness.

Given that the goodness of God went infinitely beyond man's ability to attain it, God, if He so desired, would have to come to where man was. But an incessantly good God cannot relate to a man who ceases to be good. As a result, mankind now has the ability to use for evil that which was intended for good.

There is no doubt that we have become a society that legislates and guards vice rather than virtue. We pass laws that protect our vices rather than legislation that would encourage our society to become morally upright. When a society sides with vice, it experiences consequences.

THE ROOT OF VICE IS SELF-DEIFICATION

If freedom is simply defined as having the ability to do whatever one chooses to do no matter what the cost, then we should not have any problem with industries of vice. However, we must remember there is always a cost involved with this type of societal attitude. People can harm people intentionally or unintentionally when vices are legislated and flaunted as freedoms. This seems to be a very selfish existence. Selfishness tends toward isolation and destruction, not fellowship and production.

CHAPTER SEVEN

The Gods of Sloth

THE ROAD TO SELF-DEIFICATION THROUGH ATHEISM

Historically, freedom has been more about giving and preserving than taking and destroying. That is no longer the case in our "throw away society." We use, choose, booze, ruse, and snooze all in the name of freedom, and yet in the end, freedom is the very thing we lose.

The meaning of the term freedom has gone from brotherly love to self-love. The idea of loving your neighbor as yourself has been replaced with the attitude of ignore your neighbor; love yourself. This should be no surprise for a society that has become increasingly hostile to monotheists. While at the same time, society has become increasingly open to atheists.

Why should this change? Freedom is about self-sacrifice for the preservation of others, not about self-preservation at the sacrifice of others; that latter attitude actually binds a society. Neighborly love is the key to freedom. When Jesus Christ propagated the philosophy of neighborly love, he did so with the understanding that a person can only love others as much as the source of his love allows. Christ's life was a series of exhausting attempts to point people toward the ultimate source of love. In fact, for his finale, he allowed himself to be riveted to a cross that served as an arrow pointing upward.

He made it clear that the motivating factor behind loving one's neighbor could only be stimulated by a deep-founded love for God. To clear the minds of the people of any misunderstanding, he stated that in order for a person to adequately love his neighbor as he loves himself, he needed to recognize an even more important truth, namely the need to love his God with all of his heart, soul, and mind.[55] Since he made God the source of love, he clarified the truth about loving others: it impossible to adequately love others unless a person first loved and respected God.

If a person claims that there is no God, then why should our society expect him to feel any obligation toward loving his neighbor or even himself for that matter?

This absence of a source of love makes the teaching of evolution in the classroom the paramount threat to our founders' idea of freedom. Evolution allows humans to explain their existence apart from a creator. As a result, the chief end of teaching evolution is to produce atheists. If humans can explain their existence apart from a creator, then they can live however they choose. If there is no God, then there are no absolute standards. If there are no absolute standards, we can live however we want to because there is no higher authority holding us accountable to any set of principles. Therefore, humans become god.

Logically speaking, even atheists, who conclude that the earth evolved from chance rather than that a good God created it, recognize that there had to be a time that was better than the one in which we are currently living. The essence of existence begs a logical person to reach that conclusion. There had to be a time when everything worked together at the same time in order for life not only to come into being, but also to survive without interruptions. Even in our short lives, we as humans recognize that the spawning of life is a very fragile and progressive development. When that progression is compromised or altered, survival ends.

Conversely, the very essence of survival forces a person to recognize that times have gotten worse. Why the need for survival if progress is being made? Survival is pregnant with the idea of fighting for one's life.

If you were to ask an educated person to compare something as simple as the weapons of today with the weapons of one hundred years ago, he would deduce, based on the theory of evolution, that we are creatures bent on destroying each other. As time passes, we can certainly do it faster and more efficiently. We have a habit of destroying faster than we preserve. All one has to do is study the history of nuclear energy in order to discover that we can take good things and develop weapons of mass destruction for evil. This glimpse at history is yet another proof that existence is not only threatened but becoming progressively more difficult.

Quite honestly, from an evolutionary standpoint, who can blame nations for wanting to have weapons of mass destruction, because in order to survive they have to destroy the other guy, or at least have the capability to do so, before he destroys them. This scramble for superior destructive strength is further evidence that humans are desperately evil. While there has been an evolution, it has not been positive. If anything, this evolution bears witness against us that the world and specifically the human race have not gotten gradually better as evolutionists would have us to conclude, but rather, considerably worse in a short period of time. Our weapons of choice have gone from swords that were only three feet in length to missiles that are now three stories high.

Daggers were very personal, hand-to-hand devices; a soldier would look his enemy in the eye as they both attempted to shed one another's blood. Today we do not even have to hold our daggers; we press an impersonal button to launch them. We do not look the other man in the eye; how could we when, at times, he is hundreds or even thousands of miles away? We do not feel the cold blade penetrate the warm flesh of our opponent. Instead, we incinerate thousands of men and women at a time in a matter of seconds.

The result of evolution is that its end is not warm, personal peace, which is a prerequisite for survival and development, but rather cold, impersonal war.

Two objections usually surface in an argument such as this. First, if an atheist concedes that religion apparently is necessary or beneficial for morality and, in turn, freedom, he will usually desire more proof for the existence of God. If not satisfied with the proof that is provided, most atheists, since they are uncertain of God's existence, decide to err on the side of possibility. This generally leads to some augmentation in the basic view of their surroundings, resulting in some form of agnosticism.

THE ROAD TO SELF-DEIFICATION THROUGH AGNOSTICISM

Agnosticism is the belief that there might be a higher being, but he is so far removed from us that he does not really matter. He exists, but he does not make himself known to us, and therefore, we cannot really know him. He is impersonal.

Since there may be a higher being that cannot be known, then it is assumed that his ways or standards cannot be known. Therefore, there is no way for him to expect us to know his standards. Since we can't know his standards and he can't expect us to know his standards, then it would be unfair for him to hold us accountable for violating his standards, if indeed he does exist.

Regrettably, the end of this line of thought is the same as atheism. Even though there may be a higher being that exists, whoever or whatever he is, apparently is unconcerned with the current plight of humanity; therefore humans must assume the position of deity. The key assumption in this line of thinking is that ignorance smothers consequence.

Certainly, our own world does not teach us that ignorance smothers consequence. If a woman has sexual relations with a man who is infected with the HIV virus, she can still contract the disease whether or not she knows he has the disease. Furthermore, a three-year-old who rushes out into the road to fetch his ball can be crushed by an eighteen-wheeler, whether or not he completely understands the concept of force as it relates to time and distance. Consequence does not depend upon knowledge.

A second agnostic position is much like the first but realizes the logical fallacy that accompanies the position of ignorance. In an attempt to be intellectually honest with the information, a person in this camp will endeavor to fuse creation with evolution. This fusion is known as theistic evolution. A person holding this belief evidently feels this conclusion satisfies both sides of the equation. Theistic evolution recognizes the necessity of acknowledging the divine hand behind the design, without conceding the theory of evolution. However, this attempt is like mixing water with oil. A person can place the two in the same container and even shake them together, but they never really bond and the water always separates from the oil.

Agnostics, and even some creationists, have promoted this amalgamation. When an agnostic promotes theistic evolution, it is really an attempt to make the creationist compromise his position. When a creationist or theist promotes theistic evolution, whether he realizes it or not, he is still the one compromising his position and creating an inconsistency in his view of origins.

Some theists do this in sort of an intercessory fashion. It seems as though they hope to appear intellectually honest with the cultural information and bring peaceful reconciliation to both sides. However, if they do this, they need to realize that they are still the ones who have adjusted their position. A creationist cannot maintain the integrity of his view of origins if he compromises creation in its purest form as recorded in the book of Genesis. Logically speaking, the theories of evolution and creation are mutually exclusive and incompatible.

The theory of creation and the theory of evolution must be seen as mutually exclusive because the creation account is a personal account of a personal God creating a personal and welcoming environment for His ultimate creation, mankind. Genesis is the chief source of information for the creation account. Whether one agrees with it or not, to alter Genesis is to alter the creation record. The creation account presents an intimate being overseeing his creation with order and consistency. This being is like a writer who carefully selects His words and wrestles with the syntax in order to complete a well-written book. In Genesis this being is not presented as one who leaves anything undone. He is not presented as one who simply speaks ingredients into existence and then leaves them open to chance to fall where they may throughout the rest of time. In fact, if there is indeed a designer, then chance is non-existent from his point of view. Words, or anything else for that matter, do not exist unless he speaks.

Another reason that evolution and creation are incompatible and mutually exclusive ideas is that nothing in the Genesis record of creation indicates that the account should be interpreted any other way but literally. When people attempt to add information to the text, then the text becomes diluted and meaningless. To alter the first eleven chapters of Genesis forces a person to make alterations in other passages of both the Old and New Testament as well.

In Genesis chapters 1 and 2, there are contextual phrases that are key indications that this whole episode took place over six twenty-four hour periods. The reader is presented with the dark void, and then, with just a word, God creates light. He calls the light day, the dark night and then concludes by saying, "there was evening and there was morning, one day."[56] He establishes that the standard measure of a day has to do with the amount of light. As we observe what astronomers have known for some time now, we discover that in order for the earth to sustain life, it has to expose the entire planet to a certain amount of light each day. Therefore, the earth consistently makes one rotation on its axis in a twenty-four hour period.

If a day in Genesis was to be re-interpreted as one thousand years or more[57] as some have proposed in the Day-Age theory[58], not only does this add incompatible information by making one day equal to 8,760,000 hours, but it also would have made the planet uninhabitable. With that slow of a pace, certain sections of the earth would get scorched by too much exposure to the sun's rays while others would be completely frozen. Furthermore, the earth would have had to have been much further away from the sun in order to curb the effects of the gravitational pull, which in turn would allow for a much slower rotation. This further complicates what we currently experience—a healthy planet.

The Day-Age theory complicates other aspects of creation as well. For instance, if each day was separated from one another by one thousand years, then life on the planet would be impossible during the third day-age. We are told according to the Genesis record that the sea, land and vegetation were created on the third day. On the fourth day, the sun, moon and stars are created. So according to the Day-Age theory, the plants would have had to survive one thousand years without any sunlight. Once again, this is incompatible with the current data that we are able to observe concerning plants. Plants need sunlight to survive.

Many more difficulties exist with the Day-Age theory that can be analyzed, but the outcome of atheism, agnosticism, or even theistic evolution is to lower God to an inferior position than what a literal interpretation of Scripture promotes. As a result of God's demotion, humans then receive a promotion; for the thought is that they are not as connected to or dependent upon God as was traditionally taught.

Therefore, if God is distant, impersonal, or extinct, and an individual wants to get hooked on a certain substance, who is to say that he may not do so? Since there is indeed a God, however, a person who chooses to do something outside of that which God has prescribed, has sinned. According to the Scriptures, sin is what God is not.[59] God is order; sin is chaos.[60] For a person to depend upon chaos in hopes that it will bring order to his life is sin. An attitude of independence from God produces self-deification. A person who depends upon self, will ultimately be surrounded by chaos because there are things in life that are completely out of his control, and he will self destruct.

If God exists, then there is a universal standard of morality. Morality tends to get in the way of human vice. Therefore, the best way to rid ourselves of God's morality is to rid ourselves of God or, at least, the traditional view of God.

There are some ideas that mask themselves as latent Christianity when in reality they are nothing more than ideas that stem from agnosticism. One such idea that for some reason appeals especially to people who were reared in Jewish or Christian families is the idea that there is no hell and therefore all people go to heaven. In the human mind, it seems inconceivable that God, if he does exist, would be so cruel as to punish individuals by sending them to a place called hell. While this idea seems compassionate on the surface, the underlying premise of such a belief does away with other precious doctrines that the Bible teaches, even as it excuses misbehavior.

One of those doctrines is the doctrine of sin. If there is no hell and all people go to heaven, then all people would be satisfying and pleasing in the sight of Almighty God. The result of this teaching would mean we have no explanation for the problem of evil in the world, which is dealt with almost immediately in the opening chapters of the Bible. People who promote universal salvation actually demote God's view of justice by claiming that if he does exist, he does not really care what we do to each other. Promoting such a view does not only attack God's view of justice, but it is also an attack upon his character. This is yet another attempt to bring God down to a level of human rationality.

If God is not just, then neither is he holy. Therefore, we must take him down from his pedestal because apparently, he is not much different than we are. If he is not holy, then how can we even begin to talk about his goodness? If God is not good, then why should we expect him to get involved in the fight against evil, or why should we fight it ourselves for that matter? If God is not good, then neither is he loving, and if that is the case, then we have just lost all hope for freedom or any kind of higher or enduring standard of love. There is no benevolent creator to whom we can look for direction; humanity must be our guide.

One more point must be made. If all humans go to heaven because hell does not exist, then there really are no consequences for bad behavior. If there are no consequences for bad behavior, then Jesus Christ, the very Son of God, died for no reason.[61] This idea, whether the promoters claim to be

Christians or not, renders Christianity inconsequential. Furthermore, since Orthodox Judaism is based upon the idea that humanity is inherently evil, then, it too, would be rendered meaningless.[62] We would have to conclude, if there really was no need to cleanse the evil of humanity by sending God's Son to the cross, then instead of ending up with the greatest act of God's love to mankind, we end up with the cruelest act that has ever been committed by a father to a son.

On the other hand, if God was willing to send his own Son from heaven to earth to die on a cross, do we really doubt for one moment that he will hesitate to send humans to hell for rejecting what his son did?

Without a convincing explanation for the problem of evil in the world, humanity is left with a basic philosophical quandary. People are being asked to ignore one of the basic and most verifiable problems in all of human existence. How does one deal with the issue of human cruelty? What about the villains who are clever enough to evade law enforcement, so that they are never brought to justice? Is there no ultimate authority guaranteeing that even though heinous crimes may have gone unnoticed, unreported, undiscovered, or unverified here on earth there will be an unavoidable judgment day? What reference can be used as a guide for justice? If man is the measure of justice, then which man do we follow?

The goal of evolution is atheism or agnosticism, and the end of these two philosophies is human deification. We become the drivers of our own destiny and choose to evolve into whatever we wish, with absolutely no obligation to our fellow man or to our designer. If we are not obligated to love and to serve someone outside of and higher than ourselves, then we are under no obligation to love and to serve someone outside of and equal to ourselves. God either does not exist, or he is too irresponsible or carefree to finish what he started. He set everything in motion, lost interest, and left. We evolved, and it is up to us to make the most of the situation. We have done fine for ourselves thus far, so there is absolutely no need to invite God back to work.

This line of thinking leads us to one final mistake that agnostics make. They fail to recognize that if there was a creator who set everything in motion and then left, nothing is keeping him from interfering now. If he wants to, could he not, at anytime, step in and reclaim the materials that he created in the first place? An agnostic may argue that such an action is not fair. Do we really think that an individual who is powerful enough to ignite the beginnings of life will be concerned about whether or not we think something is fair? The fact that we as humans have an understanding of fairness, does not obligate him to be fair, as we understand fairness, unless he is like us and we are like him.

We expect God to be like us if, indeed, he does exist. This is quite humorous, especially considering that one would think the thing created ought to think itself subservient and like its creator. However, this perception is not true for agnostics. They are convinced that this being has left, never to return again. This conviction is the fallacy of their faith. It leads to self-deification and human degradation. This type of existence tends toward selfishness.

As far as others are concerned, the only time a person would be obliged to help another human is when his own existence would benefit.

A pure agnostic will display likenesses to the image of his creator or, more correctly, the creator that he has imagined, whether he claims to know him or not. His creator has been generated purely from his own mind. This is a confusing scenario, for it seems as though the mind of the agnostic, in reality, is the creator of his creator. If the creator of the agnostic was negligent in leaving the project of creation undone, then it would seem to follow that the nature of the creature should be saturated with the same characteristics of the creator. It would also seem to follow that if agnostic tendencies pervaded the land then we should be able to visibly observe the effects. If the agnostic's creator was negligent in his relationship with humans, then we should see an epidemic of negligence within our society, especially within relationships. Based on this argument it is obvious as one analyzes the data on divorce that ours must be a nation that has been highly influenced by agnostic tendencies.

What does divorce have to do with agnostic ideas? Divorce rates in our society are at an all-time high compared to the recorded history of marriage.[63] The rate of divorce was not always high, which means that an ideology within the society has drastically changed. If we could pinpoint the change, then we would be able to come to some sort of conclusion about the cause.

If human beings have the ability to rationally think about their creator, then it would seem to follow that they received this ability from their creator. Regardless of how distant he was during the developing stages of humanity, the creator left an indelible mark of himself upon humanity. The ideology that has changed is that there are no ultimate consequences for neglect because there is no superior being holding us accountable for our actions.

Admittedly, not all agnostics are negligent; in fact, some are considerate, thoughtful, and even perfectionist. Creativity is defined by its source. Therefore, in order for a person to be considered creative, her work would have to be measured by the standard or source of creativity. If that source indeed is God, we can conclude she is creative as we see some part of God's creation in her. If she fails to give credit to the source of her creativity, that does not eliminate the source. The only thing it eliminates is a proper understanding of the role she plays within creation. She is not the Creator but only a creator that has been given limited creativity by her Creator. By neglecting to recognize the Creator, she has committed an error of credit. She has failed to give credit where credit is due and thus has taken the credit for herself. She has renounced her humanity and hijacked divinity.

THE ROAD TO SELF-DEIFICATION THROUGH PANTHEISM

Self-deification is not a recent development. In fact, there are many similarities between evolution and another worldview known as pantheism. Pantheism is the idea that all is God. Pantheism encompasses such religions as Hinduism and Buddhism. What does pantheism have to do with atheism, agnosticism, or vice? The most apparent parallel is self-deification. A pantheist believes that he is to become one with the universal soul. This universal soul is also referred to as the impersonal god or force. This force drives and determines everything. The goal of humanity is to tap into the power of the force by becoming one with it.

A human becomes one with the impersonal soul by emptying himself of all personality. He is to become like the impersonal universal soul. In order to accomplish this, he practices breathing exercises in different postural positions and, at times, says recorded prayers, also called mantras. This exercise is known as yoga. It is supposed to relax the body and rejuvenate the mind while thinking upon nothing. This is the path to ultimate assimilation with the universe. Once this metamorphosis is complete, the human becomes one with the all-encompassing universal soul. This state is known as nirvana.

Pantheists believe that human beings are divine manifestations of the universal soul or force. Once nirvana is achieved, a person can be promoted to the next level in this assimilation process by becoming a spiritual master. A spiritual master is one who helps other people achieve nirvana. He does this by manipulating reality, not only his reality, but also the reality of others. This certainly can be viewed as another parallel to evolution because evolutionists purport that human beings have the ability to manipulate their surroundings through intelligence. Supposedly through evolution, organisms thought their way through to the next level of development. Pantheists allege that human beings have the ability to manipulate their surroundings through a higher knowledge.

Within this ideology, reality becomes illusion. Nothing is real; everything is relative. The only reality is impersonal assimilation with the universal soul. Everything is neither good nor bad; everything just is. The only sin is when a person embraces his personality. Basically, the person who is furthest away from the true reality is the person who fails to recognize that there is no reality. Anything personal or physical is just an illusion. All that this world has to offer by way of individual expression is keeping a person from the ultimate expression, namely to become one with the impersonal, universal impression. Doing something considered morally wrong has no physical consequence for a person because the physical realm does not exist. The only consequence is that it stalls a person's spiritual journey to complete assimilation with the universe.

Once again, in the pantheistic model, as was seen in the atheistic and agnostic models, humans become the drivers of their destiny, manipulating reality in whatever way they choose with no obligation to their fellow man. Once a person recognizes that his goal in life is to become one with the universe, there is no obligation to his neighbor. On the surface, this worldview seems very selfless, others-centered or even universe-centered. However, when one probes deeper, it becomes clear that this idea is the very core of self-centeredness. A pantheist is released from any obligations or responsibilities because his surroundings, whether they are animate or inanimate, are equal illusions. He who has achieved the greatest level of assimilating self holds the keys to this path. He who holds the keys to this path will have achieved the greatest ability to manipulate others.

Even a pantheist, at this point, might argue that he does not relinquish his physical obligations. He might even give some specific examples of the responsibilities that he faithfully maintains. For instance, he may be a loving husband or a good father. After applauding a pantheist who is a loving husband or a good father, it might be a good idea to ask him why he maintains these responsibilities. If everything moral is relative and everything physical an illusion, maybe an even better question might be, "How do you define words such as *loving*, *husband*, *good*, or *father*?" How is it that we are even able to use physical symbols to communicate and ask these questions? Maybe he maintains his responsibilities because it provides the greatest amount of freedom for him within the physical realm. Maybe he maintains his responsibilities so that he will have a greater impact upon the people who value the maintenance of physical responsibilities. As a result, this success may grant him more opportunities to share his faith. Regardless of the reason that a pantheist gives, if anything in his daily life reveals that he values the physical or personal realms, he is not being forthright with his ideology. His lifestyle is contradicted.

However, a pantheist would probably be quick to point out that since there is no real value to the physical or personal realms, the contradiction does not matter. What a non-pantheist views as a contradiction, the pantheist does not since physical aspects of the universe are an illusion. Everything that is, is swallowed up by everything else.

An apparent contradiction is not a big deal to some. In essence, ideas, emotions and behaviors do not always have to be either right or wrong; they can be both right and wrong or they can just be. This concept evidently ignores the law of non-contradiction upon which logic so heavily depends.

This worldview, from a physical standpoint, becomes illogical because a pantheist would argue there is no physical. Even though science and experience have shown that the mental depends upon the physical just as the physical depends upon the mental, pantheists insist that the physical is an illusion. Apparently it does not occur to them that they are moving their tongues and air from their lungs over their lips producing a physical sound that must reverberate upon an eardrum and be processed by another's cerebrum.

Since to their way of thinking there is no physical, it becomes impossible to define any type of mental boundaries for freedom. Therefore, their ideology becomes irrefutable. They are right no matter what a person may argue.

Unfortunately, this view of the world is not very practical or comforting. How does one comfort a continent of people who just lost over one hundred thousand lives, a third of whom were children, due to an unexpected tsunami? How does one comfort an individual mother who lost all of her children due to this unexpected act of God? As she weeps for her children, what person in his right mind would try to console her by saying, "Don't worry. The relationship that you had with your children was not real anyway." Some pantheist may argue that this assertion is an unfair treatment of the overall worldview and that it is too sweeping in its allegations, but the fact is that this is the practical end of all pantheistic thought. The only way for pantheistic thought to become practical is to assimilate itself with another worldview that contradicts pantheism itself.

THE ROAD TO SELF-DEIFICATION THROUGH MONOTHEISM

For the sake of prudence, let us turn our attention to the last major view. Thus far we have dealt with atheism, which states that there must not be a god. As a result of this mentality, the atheist becomes the designer of his reality choosing to indulge in whatever vice he wants. Next we dealt with agnosticism which states that there might be a god. As a result of this view of the world, the agnostic still places himself in the position of reality designer because there is absolutely no obligation on his part to succumb to a god who is absent from reality. This view does little more than give academic credence to the possibility of there being a god. Lastly we surveyed some of the key concepts of pantheism and found that the ultimate goal is to become one with the universe in order to achieve the status of a spiritual master and manipulate apparent reality of self and society. This view once again places the adherent in a position to be the designer of his reality. The time has now come to deal with the view that purports there must be a God.

Atheism, agnosticism, and pantheism are not the only religions, which are prone to self-deification. Admittedly, even some monotheists have vices to which they are addicted. However, at least the monotheist can logically recognize that he has an inconsistency with his worldview. On the one hand, he says that he believes in a God who must exist and will hold him accountable for his actions. On the other hand, his actions communicate that he is living as if there is not a God. He claims that there is a just God but lives as if there is not. God is there, but he does not care. Failure to pay homage to the creator would be like failing to pay a landlord, and we all know the results when that happens. One could justifiably point out that a monotheist or theist who lives this way is behaviorally an agnostic. This inconsistence proves that a person's worldview hinges upon his practical behavior and not upon his verbal creeds.

It is interesting to note that most views of God attempt to complicate or obscure the relationship between God and man. However practical, daily living teaches us that the most enjoyable relationships are the least complicated. For example, a mother who desires to have a healthy relationship with her little girl does not intentionally avoid her. Neither does she make it difficult for the little girl to love her, even though the mother's intelligence far exceeds the daughter's. Certainly, this simplicity in human relationships must stem from somewhere. When two humans are easily able to relate to one another, that is a relationship that is destined for deep love.

A person's true beliefs then can be determined by his consistent behavior, especially within relationships. A self-declared monotheist can behave like an agnostic. And a self-declared atheist can behave as if there is a higher being who holds him accountable to an absolute standard of morality. In either case, these people are behaving in a manner that is in contradiction to their stated beliefs. Since the standards for right and wrong are constantly shifting under the guises of atheism and agnosticism, we need to examine if the same rings true for monotheism.

CHAPTER EIGHT

ADAM AND EVE AND ABRAHAM'S SEED

IN SEARCH OF VIRTUE

LET US EXAMINE the three major monotheistic religions of the world to see if we can determine if there are any stable and universal moral standards for virtue, responsibility, and ultimately freedom. This examination will be brief and in no way will attempt to analyze every doctrine within a given faith. Since these religions have had so much interaction throughout history, they will be dealt with comparatively in this section. If it can be determined that there are universal moral standards, then we should also be able to determine which religion promotes the greatest amount of freedom for the greatest number of people. If this can be determined, then certainly our society would do well to adhere to the tenets of this faith, especially since a society without the right religion cannot maintain any stable or moral accountability. The three monotheistic religions are Islam, Judaism, and Christianity.

ISLAM

The first of the three religions that we will deal with is Islam. What does Islam offer in the way of freedom? In order to answer this question we must first take a brief look at the origin of Islam and then examine whether or not the tenets of this faith produce freedom or bondage, not only for its faithful, but also for others.

The Islamic system of belief came into being about A.D. 600. It began in the mind of a man named Mohammed, who claimed, after some persuasion from his older wife, that an angel had appeared to him while he was alone in a cave. Mohammed claimed he received revelation that there was no other god but Allah and that he was his sole prophet. It should be noted that he could have easily been exposed to the surrounding religions of Judaism and Christianity, possibly by his uncle who raised him after the deaths of his parents. Although he claimed to have great respect for these religions, he also claimed that the writings of their prophets had been tainted. He taught his followers that he accepted all of the biblical prophets but not the way that their writings had been passed down throughout the preceding centuries.

Since his hometown of Mecca was an epicenter of civilization that welcomed many gods who were displayed upon a mammoth rock known today as the Ka'bah, it is no surprise that Mohammed quickly gained a following for his newly-founded monotheistic religion. People generally welcomed any addition to the pantheon of gods. Apparently there was an understanding among the people that allowed them to serve their given idol as long as they did not offend anybody by claiming exclusive truth. Mohammed's idea was unpopular with many of the local merchants, however, because their primary source of income was from the pilgrims who traveled to Mecca in order to trade goods and offer gifts to their many gods. Therefore, from their perspective, when Mohammed, a businessman before and after devoting his life solely to Allah, claimed there was only one true god he alone represented, those merchants concluded he was attempting to monopolize their industry and, thus, steal their business.[64] Because of this, Mohammed and his followers (numbering about one hundred people) were driven out of town.

By violent force, they established themselves in the nearby city of Medina. After a short period, they eventually went back to Mecca and, through a series of battles, took over the city. This pattern of conquest became a trademark of the Muslims, as they would come to be known. To their credit, the Muslims did initially offer asylum to Jews and Christians who also occupied the cities that they had taken over. This friendship, however, was tenuous at best and quickly changed when those of other faiths were given an ultimatum either to endorse and embrace Islam as the authentic religion, "pay continuous compensation for Islamic protection," or die by the sword.[65]

Although Mohammed, and his followers after him, claimed they embraced all the biblical prophets, they also claimed the writings of the prophets had been corrupted. This was, no doubt, an attempt to recognize the weight of the biblical writings without having to embrace them as truth. Muslims to this day claim to esteem some of the writings of Moses, David, the prophets, and even the Gospels. However, no matter how highly they claim to venerate them, they still assert that these writings have been tainted, and therefore they do not adhere to them. Thus they claim that Mohammed has become the sole authority concerning divine revelation.

Therefore, it seems obvious that initially Mohammed and his followers patronized believers of the Jewish and Christian faiths in order to attract them to the idea of peaceful coexistence with their Muslim friends who were quickly gaining strength. This apparent tolerance would still allow Mohammed to maintain his position behind the wheel of revelatory history. By claiming that the prophetic record of the Bible had been tainted, Mohammed, established himself as the only true prophet. One item that he apparently neglected in claiming the unreliability of the Biblical text, however, was manuscript evidence.

In fact, today scholars have accumulated well over twenty-four thousand manuscripts of the New Testament alone. Some of these date back to at least three centuries before Mohammed. There have even been some fragmented portions of the Gospels that date back to within fifty years of their origin.[66] If these documents had been tainted or corrupted, it would seem to follow that the loyal followers of Jesus Christ at that time would have spoken out against such, but there is no evidence to indicate inaccurate texts was an early church issue.

Apparently it is Mohammed's record that is tainted. To date there is in fact not one shred of manuscript evidence prior to Mohammed that validates the Koran. If Mohammed's doctrinal treatise was true in stating that the biblical record was tainted, then there would always remain the possibility of finding some ancient document to validate his claim. However, there is no such evidence, at least none found to date.

Are we expected to believe that the true revelation of God was completely obliterated from history? Is God not strong enough to accurately maintain his message throughout time? Is he solely dependent upon human integrity to pass the ancient scrolls from one generation to the next? Absolutely not. In fact, this idea would even violate the Islamic doctrine of transmission. Are we to believe that the Biblical record is so tainted that only trace elements exists from what was originally recorded? There are not too few documents to examine; in fact they are in abundance. Historians, archaeologists, and scholars add to the collection every year. Instead of finding great discrepancies, they find uniform agreement across the span of time and linguistic differences. Mohammed's revelation is in no way supported by the writings of Moses, the Prophets, or the Apostles. The writings of Mohammed stand completely alone. His so-called revelation is an example of self-authentication.

Mohammed would have us believe that there was some massive conspiracy that took place over a period of fifteen hundred years (or two thousand years, including his lifetime), which was the amount of time it took to complete both the Old and New Testaments. This alleged conspiracy involved over forty different men who agreed to the plot, though more times than not they were separated by time and space.

If there is one thing we have discovered about human fallacies, it is that they have a tendency to become obvious over time, especially when they involve conspiracies. This distortion of the truth usually becomes clear because one or more of the participants slips under the pressure to maintain the story.

Islam's inaccurate representation of the Bible not only violates our second qualification of freedom, which is a responsibility to tell the truth, it also violated Jewish Law, which existed for two thousand years prior to Mohammed, and Christian doctrine. Both state that one's testimony is only considered valid if confirmed by two or three witnesses. Consequently, Jews and Christians would not subject themselves to an individual such as Mohammed who was ignoring their prophetic records. These records were not only confirmed by two or three witnesses but by more than two or three million, over a period of two or three millennia. In fact, both Jews and Christians believe this man was blaspheming the Word of God, which in part explains why there is so much conflict between these groups.

Scriptural integrity rests upon the shoulders of history. In fact, the two are inseparable. Scripture cannot exist without history, and history cannot exist without Scripture. Scripture preserves history in the same way that history has preserved Scripture. Scriptural integrity cannot be compromised by the passage of time because it is tied up with history. One of the major strengths of Scripture is that it remains unscathed throughout history. Scripture has endured the test of time, and time can even be used to test how well it has endured.[67] Every time another ancient manuscript or artifact is discovered, it serves to prove the impeccable integrity of the biblical record.

One example when Scripture preserved history (for the biblical record indeed is history) is the account of Pontius Pilate. This man was the primary authority who oversaw the prosecution of Jesus Christ. In the past, his existence has been debated by scholars because the only mention of his name was within the Gospel record. Some historians contended that since there was no other historical mention of this man, it must be concluded that he did not exist. In their line of thinking, he did not exist until proven otherwise. Logic would dictate that history should embrace his existence until evidence to the contrary surfaced, but this approach was not followed in this case.

Some people approach the existence of God in the same way. If they question the existence of God, they certainly will not have reservations about questioning the existence of a man.

In the case of Pilate's existence, Italian archaeologists in 1961 discovered his name chiseled into a limestone block while excavating a Roman amphitheater located near the port city of Caesarea.[68] The professional conclusion was that the slab dated to the time of Jesus Christ.

Another related point of tension with which Christians take issue is that Muslims begin their prayers with the statement that there is no other god but Allah, and Mohammed is his prophet. Christians are taught by Jesus Christ himself to open their prayers by saying, "Our Father which art in heaven, hallowed is thy name."[69] Jesus also said to his followers in another passage that if they were to ask anything in his name it would be granted.[70] As a result, Christians pray to the Heavenly Father in Jesus' name. According to Christian doctrine, the sacrificial death and victorious resurrection of Jesus Christ make it possible for the believer to approach the throne of heaven. To claim to do so by any other means or name is considered blasphemy.

Christians believe that in order to pray to God, one has to approach God with the authority of someone who is equal to God, namely through Jesus Christ. Therefore, from a Christian's perspective, when Muslims pray to Allah, it appears as if they are approaching Allah by the authority of Mohammed's name. Since Christians view Jesus Christ as divine, they believe that it is his authority that allows them to approach God. Even though Muslims claim there is no other god but Allah, they appear to elevate Mohammed to the level of divinity by ascribing authority to him. Since his name is mentioned in the same breath and on the same level with their god, it appears as though he has achieved deity. Therefore, in the Muslim mind, whether they admit this or not, Mohammed is exalted above every other prophet including Jesus Christ and is, therefore, equal to God.[71]

One final thought about Islam as it relates to self-deification: if one had the opportunity to ask a Muslim where he would go after he dies, he would respond that only Allah knows for certain. This response seems to have some of the same nuances as agnosticism. The only difference is that instead of saying that there might be a god, Muslims state there is indeed a god; however, one cannot truly know for certain whether or not an individual has a reservation in heaven. Allah is a transcendent god, and his subjects must satisfy him by producing more good works than bad ones. However, Allah is the only one who knows whether or not a person's good deeds have outweighed his evil deeds over his lifetime. Even human relationships demonstrate that when a person is subject to another person, if he does not know what is expected of him, or how well he is doing, this uncertainty has a tendency of producing frustration and confusion in the submissive party. This type of ambiguity not only leads one to question the value of his existence, but it also ends up producing a fatalistic view of the world. People do desperate things in order to receive the approval of someone who is difficult to please.

What is more, a Muslim has to deal with the attributes ascribed to god. But how do love and security apply? Love and security are two of the most essential needs in the life of every human; they are the basis for freedom and peace of mind. The truest virtues of love are not based upon merit but upon something much deeper. If a person loves another only for the benefit he receives, and the object of his love ceases to perform, then he will no longer love that person.

This situation can be compared to a high school relationship in which a girl is dating a quarterback with a promising future in college football. She has enjoyed the attention showered upon him from fans and scouts alike. But one day during a big game, he gets sacked by an opponent, and to the horror of the fans, he does not get up. He complains that he cannot move his hands or feet. Later he learns he will never be able to walk again. From his girlfriend's point of view, the relationship will never be what it once was. She decides she is too young to care for a paralytic the rest of her life and ends the relationship. Most people may understand her decision. Other people may accuse her of being an opportunist who abandoned her boyfriend when he needed her the most. In her mind she may rationalize that he will be taken care of by his parents and that she need not waste anymore of her time. So she leaves, taking with her any elements of love and security he thought existed between them.

This young paralyzed man went from a life of above average athletic ability and attention to a life that is now restricted to a chair he controls with his mouth. As he clumsily manipulates his joystick, he thinks, what a sorry excuse of an existence. He begins to think of how loved and how promising his future once was compared to how unlovely he feels now. But he has forgotten one group of people who have loved him from the moment he was conceived: his parents. Their love for him is not based upon merit. They loved him when he could do nothing for himself. They will still love him now. Their love for him was never based upon his athletic ability or his physical utility; it was based upon the fact that he was their child.

If humans can love their children regardless of their limitations, certainly God can. If God exists, then humans must have received this ability from their designer. When we look at God's handiwork, it seems ridiculous to think that we humans can do something that is god-worthy, something that will gain his approving nod. If we could do something equal to his, it would seem that his approval would be unnecessary. His level of achievement would not be beyond ours. If his level of achievement is something we can attain apart from his assistance, then either he is not needed, does not exist, is a human, or we are gods capable of doing what he has done.

So once again, we have a worldview that intends to produce virtue for its adherents but falls short. Islam lacks definitive boundaries in the realm of understanding the deity in relation to humanity. The end result is a dramatic reduction in the value of human life. The founder of Islam elevated himself above all earthly authorities—past, present, or future—by claiming to hold the keys to eternity. This is indeed the epitome of self-deification because he alleged to be the way to god, asserting that no man comes to Allah except through Mohammed's writings, and thus placing himself on par with God.[72] It would be interesting to know whether or not Mohammed himself was certain of his eternal destination. Or if he too would simply respond, "As Allah wills, so it will be."

JUDAISM

The next monotheistic religion that has had a profound influence upon the rest of the world is Judaism. It is impossible to talk about Judaism without talking about the nation of Israel. Their holy book is none other than the Hebrew Scriptures. These holy writings have endured through times of instability and uncertainty. Probably one of the greatest enigmas of Judaism is its ability to survive regardless of what has happened to the nation of Israel. Historically, Israel is among the smallest nations, but its influence has been among the greatest. No other nation in history has enjoyed more time in the spotlight than the nation of Israel. While other nations boast of literature and architecture that date back for centuries, Israel humbly displays its antiquity dating back three millennia.

So what is it that has allowed Israel to enjoy such longevity? Like the Muslims, has it been their great military strength? No. Although Israel has had a strong military at various times, at other periods its treasures have been ransacked, its buildings razed, its people murdered, and its existence destroyed. The Jewish people have been exiled from their land, enslaved by their captors, brought back, policed by other nations, and harassed within their own land.

So what is it that has allowed these people to endure? Many Jews would answer by saying that their Holy Scriptures have endured, thus granting them endurance. They find life and hope in the future because of what their Scriptures promise them. These people who put their hope in their sacred writings are not naïve or ignorant. In fact, some of the greatest minds that God has ever created are Jewish, and they have contributed to and influenced every branch of the arts and sciences.

When other nations have fallen or have been forgotten, what has allowed Israel to endure? Other nations have been stronger for a time, but none have lasted longer, nor have they held to a single identity. The people of Israel, in contrast, identify themselves as God's chosen people, the key players in the Jewish Scriptures. Obviously, something about them sets them apart, for countless times their identity has been challenged and jeopardized. History records the numerous times the best of their men and women have been enslaved or exterminated and their possessions stolen or destroyed. But the Jews still endure. The nation of Israel has been ridiculed and toppled by other nations, but somehow they still enjoy center stage both politically, religiously, and philosophically.

Jewish people have been known to be a virtuous and hospitable people, and they continue to be so to this day. Many Jews embrace their strong ethnic background derived from the history recorded within their Holy Scriptures. No doubt, the greatest and most influential characters in history, and the strongest, most intelligent, and most holy, are recorded in this book—men and women such as Noah, Abraham, Isaac, Jacob, Joseph, Moses, Aaron, Joshua, Samson, Samuel, David, Solomon, Elijah, Daniel, Sarah, Rebekah, Rachel, Hannah, Abigail, Ruth, and Esther.

So how have individuals like these contributed to freedom? Since they seem to overcome adversity even when faced with insurmountable odds, their example is instructive. Their resilience comes from a firmly rooted belief in God—not just any God but the one true God identified in their Scriptures.

The Jewish Scriptures contain the account of Adam and Eve and how they offended God with their disobedience in the Garden of Eden. God drove them out of the garden and told them they would be, among other things, cursed with the pain of death. At the same time, he also promised a seed that would come from Eve, whose heel would be bruised by the venomous serpent of sin but who would crush the venomous serpent of death with the antiserum of his life.[73]

The God of the Hebrew Scriptures makes it clear that sin is what He is not, and He deals with it in serious ways. Since all people are descended from Adam and Eve, all people have inherited their characteristic of sin. Within a few generations the entire population had become so poisoned by sin that their thoughts were continually evil. God in his displeasure sent a universal flood. Only Noah and his family were spared because Noah was righteous in God's estimation.[74] Noah's sons were told to propagate and fill the earth. Rather than fill the earth, their immediate descendants decided to congregate and make a name for themselves in Babel. God eventually scattered them by scrambling their universal language into many different languages.[75] As a result, this inability to communicate led to segregation.

At this point, Scripture introduces us to Abraham, the father of the Jewish faith, referred to as a friend of God.[76]Abraham is the same man Muslims claim as the father of their faith. However, claims are worthless without evidence, and the oldest evidence (some of which predates Islam by two thousand years) in this case makes it unmistakably clear that Abraham is the father of the Jewish faith.

According to the Scriptures, Abraham withheld nothing from God, not even his promised son. After the birth of the promised son of his old age, God tested Abraham. He was instructed to take his son and offer him as a sacrifice on Mount Moriah.[77] Abraham completely trusted God not only with his life but also with his son's. As a result, after he had prepared the altar and split the wood, he bound his promised son, Isaac, and lifted his knife to slay him. God waited until the last possible moment to release Abraham from the task. As a result of that test, Scripture records that God knew that this man truly feared him. Since Abraham withheld nothing from God, God would withhold nothing from Abraham. In fact, Abraham would receive a freedom from which the whole world would eventually benefit.

From this test forward, Abraham was not only given the promises of God, but he was also referred to as a friend of God. Abraham trusted God, and his faith was the necessary component in God's economy to count Abraham as righteous in his eyes.[78] One of the things God promised Abraham was that the nations of the earth would be blessed through his seed.[79] As a sign of this promise, Abraham and all of the males of his household had to be circumcised.[80] This was a very personal sign. Since the promised seed would pass through the descendants of Abraham, apparently circumcision was the best reminder. Any time a Jewish male was unclothed, the sight of his nakedness would remind him that the promised seed could possibly come from him. As a result, he would also be held accountable to a higher standard. Any time he had the urge to behave in an immoral manner, he could not help but be reminded of the eternal covenant that his maker had made with his father.

Not only did Abraham carry out this sign, he also taught his children to circumcise their sons as well. Apparently, this practice continued all the way to the time of Moses. Scholars tell us that according to the Hebrew Scriptures, Moses and Abraham were separated by about seven hundred years.[81]

Moses was a man used by God at a time when the descendants of Abraham needed a deliverer. Israel found itself enslaved by Egypt. God used Moses to free these slaves with such power that this episode is referred to throughout the rest of the Scriptures more frequently than any other instance. According to the Scriptures, since the Egyptians would not allow the Jewish people to taste freedom, God used Moses to subject them to a series of ten plagues. The last plague was the one that broke Pharaoh's will and heart, for it claimed the life of his firstborn son.[82]

Prior to the last plague, Moses was told by God to instruct all of the families of Israel to gather their households and hastily eat a meal of lamb and unleavened bread. Furthermore, they were required to take the blood of the lamb and use it to stain the lintel and the posts on the main door of the house. If God saw the blood on the main door of the house, he passed over the house; but if there was no blood, he would claim the life of the firstborn son.[83] The children of Israel did as they were instructed. The Egyptians, on the other hand, experienced a plague so specific they could not deny that the wrath of the God of Israel was against them. In that one night, every Egyptian family experienced the loss of their firstborn son, but every firstborn Jewish male whose doorframe was stained with the blood of the lamb was spared.

The Biblical account states that Pharaoh allowed Moses and the Israelites to leave the next day. Soon after, he changed his mind and pursued Israel with his army to bring them back. The Israelites should have been easy prey for the mighty Egyptian army. All their efforts to escape must have seemed futile. Not only were the Egyptians pursuing from behind, they had no place to go because the Red Sea lay in front of them. Something miraculous happened. The sea opening up right in front of them. God provided a dry path for them right through the sea. The sea swallowed the entire Egyptian army, however, and they were drowned.[84] The children of Israel made it freely to the other side. No explanation apart from a miracle can explain how these former slaves overcame the strength of the Egyptian dynasty and lived to talk about it for generations to come.

Moses is credited with recording all that happened to the children of Israel for a period of about forty years after the freedom experienced at the Red Sea. He also received the Hebrew Law from God on Mount Sinai, a noted event in the history of freedom. The Hebrew Law, more commonly known as the Ten Commandments, involves a detailed covenant that God made with the Jewish people. If they were careful to observe the commandments as explained in the text, along with practical examples of daily life, then they would be blessed above all nations. However, if the Jewish people failed to observe the laws of this covenant, they would be cursed by God.[85] One interesting note about Moses is found in the book of Deuteronomy in chapter eighteen. He reiterates the promise that was first given to Adam and Eve and then more specifically to Abraham about a seed that was to come. In this instance, however, instead of referring to a "seed," he mentioned a prophet who would come and would be like

Moses, himself.[86] After Moses died, the children of Israel, led by Joshua, took possession of the land that was promised to Abraham some seven hundred years earlier.

An interesting observation must be noted here. In the Scriptures, a definite theme is developing around the sacrifice of the firstborn. Where did this idea first present itself? In the opening chapters of Genesis, one can see this theme unfolding. Abel, the second son of Adam and Eve, was credited for offering the firstborn of his flock to God.[87] Later Abraham was commanded by God to offer to God his firstborn son from his legitimate marriage. Moses commanded the Israelites to offer a lamb in place of their firstborn son.

However, the first instance of sacrifice recorded in Scripture came after the sin of Adam and Eve in the garden, though the account does not provide us with much detail. God made a sacrifice of animals to provide a covering for the man and his wife.[88] Because of sin man would now have to die or make a sacrifice in order to stand in the presence of and commune with God. However, in this case we find that God is the one who made the sacrifice. Why? This point may be the key to man's freedom. God has such a strong desire to commune with these beings He created, He is willing to go so far as to make a sacrifice for them. He did not have to, but out of a creator's love, He decided that instead of sacrificing or annihilating Adam and Eve, He would choose a substitute, in this case, an animal. Before sin, no sacrifice was needed. Disobedience to God constituted sin, and the penalty for sin by God's own word was death.[89] The skins that God provided Adam and Eve as a result of this sacrifice only provided temporary protection from the elements. While obedient to God, there was no need for protection from the elements. After the disobedience, protection was essential, for now Adam and Eve were mortal because they refused the instruction of the immortal one.

God's desire from this point on was to eradicate sin, as seen in the promise of the seed that would one day come to crush the serpent who instigated sin in the first place. God provided a temporary covering for Adam and Eve through the sacrifice of animals, but in time, He would provide a more permanent one through a human. We are told in Genesis 3:15 that even the seed of Eve would have to sacrifice His heel in the process of crushing the serpent.

After the time of Joshua, four hundred more years would elapse before Israel would enjoy her first king. This ruler, although a figure larger than life, was not the promised seed or the prophet like Moses who was to come.[90] But his administration did yield to a prominent and charismatic king by the name of David, recognized as the most significant ruler in Israel's history. He also received a promise from God—that his kingdom would be an everlasting kingdom. He was promised that an heir would descend from his line who would sit on his throne forever.[91] This promise was not only a reiteration of the promise that was made to Abraham and renewed through Moses, but the details of this promise provided more information as to what type of person they should expect.

They knew from the account of Adam and Eve that the promised one would fearlessly sacrifice himself (or his heel) in order to set things right. They also knew that the promised seed would be a descendant of Abraham who would bless the nations. From Moses, Israel was told this promised one would arise as a prophet among his people. And finally, through the promise given to King David, the children of Israel would know to be looking for a descendent in the line of the king. This heir became recognized in Jewish history as "the Promised One" or the Messiah.

For the next four hundred years, there was turmoil and upheaval within the Davidic line as the kingdom split and the throne changed hands numerous times. David's descendants, for the most part, maintained his kingdom until the rise of the Babylonian Empire when it was dismantled and the people deported. However, they still had hope that one day the Promised One would come.[92] A group known as prophets kept this hope alive.

The prophets provided a growing body of information about the Messiah. The prophet Daniel, for instance, foresaw him riding victoriously upon the clouds.[93] The prophet Isaiah foresaw him as a suffering and sacrificial servant who would be punished not only for the sins of Israel but also for the sins of the entire world.[94] Jeremiah the prophet foretold of a new covenant that would be established by this righteous branch of David that cleanses all from sin.[95] Many of these prophets, as well as others who are not mentioned here, declared that the coming Messiah was not just for Israel but also for the entire world. Since the entire world needed deliverance from sin, anyone who was willing could attach himself or herself to the Messiah simply by believing that he could, indeed, deliver them. Isaiah, Micah and Zechariah are just a few of the prophets who specifically mention "that many nations will join themselves to the LORD."[96]

The point in disseminating all this history recorded in the Hebrew Scriptures is that the legal covenant formulated under

Moses by the giving of the Law was and is good.[97] However, the code that Moses received was just another way of pointing out the imperfection in humanity when contrasted with God's perfection.[98] Ultimately it pointed forward to the hope that was to come.[99] The Law given to Moses was not the means to freedom or deliverance. It was just a diagnosis stating that all people were in bondage. To say the law can cure us from the ultimate disease, which is death, is like saying a doctor who has diagnosed cancer has cured his patient. He has not. He has simply identified the problem. This can be argued by the fact that the law did not even eradicate sin nor did it save Moses from death. So even he looked forward to another prophet to deliver the Jewish people, and they are still looking for their deliverer today. In conclusion, the Law, as given to Moses, made it clear that human beings were desperately evil and in need of someone to deliver them from their desperate state. They themselves could not keep the law. Consequently there was need of a new covenant.[100]

God's standards for human behavior are high because He is measure, and He is perfect. It is impossible for sinful humans to keep the standards of a holy God unless God purges us from our sinful condition.[101] In order for us to be set free from the chains of sin, He has to do it; otherwise it cannot be done. For whatever reason, He longs to do so in order to maintain a relationship with us.

Humans are under the power and persuasion of sin, which means that evil is more powerful than humans.[102] The Law itself bears witness against humanity by declaring that we are weak and in desperate need of repair. Therefore, in order to be free we need something more powerful than evil to free us from its grasp. The Law reveals that evil is more powerful than humans but that God is more powerful than evil. The Law reveals that we are powerless but God is powerful. We are hopeless, but He is our hope. We are weak, but He is strong.

The virtuous God gave humanity the Hebrew Law. The Law, or the Hebrew Covenant, acts as the scaffolding of the New Covenant. During the construction of a building, the scaffolding is essential in order to bring the work to completion. Scaffolding allows welds to be made, nails to be hammered, and bricks to be laid. After the construction is completed however, the scaffolding is taken down as if it was never there. To say that the scaffolding was irrelevant or unnecessary would be a great disservice to the men and women who used it in order to construct the building in the first place. Without the scaffolding, the building would not exist, and without the building, the scaffolding would not have been needed. However, it simply is not economically feasible for contractors to set up scaffolding unless they are in the process of building something that requires it. The sole purpose of scaffolding is to provide a large support system that allows the workers to rise to the next level of construction. As scaffolding is to the building, so the Old Covenant is to the New. Both are necessary and so tied up with each other that one could not exist without the other. The New Covenant grew out of the Old. The New Covenant was the construction that was going on behind the veil of the Old. Once the building of the New was completed, the scaffolding of the Old was taken down to reveal God's majestic work. The Hebrew Law points to the New Covenant or the New Testament.[103]

CHRISTIANITY

The final monotheistic religion is Christianity. We dealt with Islam and determined that it did not even come into existence until six centuries after Christianity. We looked into Judaism; however, we cannot understand Christianity without understanding the need for Messiah (or the promised seed), explained beautifully within the Hebrew Scriptures. One could argue that the need for Messiah is the theme of the Hebrew Scriptures. Not a need for Messiah apart from God, but a need for a Messiah who was intimately acquainted with God unlike any other anointed deliverer before him—a deliverer who would not just deliver the Jewish people from a terrestrial, political empire, but one who would deliver mankind from a sinister and ethereal dominance.

Christianity was not founded by a group of outsiders who thought it would be a good idea to manipulate much of the Hebrew Scriptures for the sake of developing a new religion. Nothing could be further from the truth. Christianity realizes the Messiah desired by the Jewish people. It does this in a variety of ways. First and foremost, Jesus Christ is not only the central figure in Christianity, but he is also a Jew.[104] He was not just any Jew; he was an expert in the Hebrew Scriptures. According to Luke, Jesus, at the age of twelve, astounded the Jewish Rabbis through his questions and comments in the temple.[105] As he entered his thirties, he began his own circuit where he primarily met Jewish people from all walks of life who followed him.

His followers consisted of men, women, and children from upper and lower classes,[106] Most were orthodox Jews who were well taught in the Hebrew Scriptures since it was mandated from the time of Moses that parents teach their children the Scriptures when they woke up in the morning, as they walked along together throughout the day, and as they lay down at night.[107] The Jews were so well acquainted with their holy scrolls that they could identify a false prophet quickly. Jesus' followers were men and women who attended weekly services in their local synagogues, listening to scribes read and explain passages from the entirety of the Scriptures.[108] They were familiar with the Law, the Writings, and the Prophets of the Scriptures.

These Jews not only read and learned the Hebrew Scriptures, but they also lived them out in the daily routine of life. They embraced Jesus because he demonstrated, more than any other teacher, how practical the Scriptures were for all areas of daily living and personal character development. His followers saw in Jesus the hope for which they had been waiting. He taught as one having authority and yet healed the infirmities of the common man.[109] He was more acceptable to the people than the scribes because he accepted the people regardless of their status.[110]

These men and women came from different backgrounds. According to the Scriptures, fishermen and tax collectors, scribes and priests, Pharisees and Sadducees (two prominent religious sects at the time of Christ), synagogue officials and soldiers, young and old, rich and poor, male and female, Jew and foreigner, the healthy and the sick all followed Christ. To be sure, some followed to see what He was going to say or do. Still others followed in order that they might debate Him. But all recognized Him as someone who was worthy of listening to because of His teachings and His actions.[111]

Even His enemies came to listen to Him. No doubt they did this so that they could test Him in the areas of academics, politics, and theology.[112] Some of His opponents eventually became true followers.[113] Still others became all the more annoyed when they tested Jesus because He responded to their questions with answers they had not considered. Most of His enemies came from the established Jewish sects of the Pharisees and Sadducees. These men had students of their own who were being drawn to Jesus, and they did not like it. They thought by engaging him publicly and in numbers they would be able to silence him.

When His enemies realized they could not prevail, history records that they took more drastic measures by manipulating the authorities into executing Him after a mock trial.[114] These Jewish leaders not only understood and spoke the same language as Jesus, they also understood their law better than any other group at that time. They understood perfectly what Jesus was claiming when he referred to Himself as the Son of God. As they clearly stated, He was making himself to be equal with God.[115] Jesus never denied this charge even when faced with the inevitability of death. As passionate as He was at defending a proper understanding of the person of God, it would have been completely out of character for Him to allow such a grave misunderstanding if indeed it was not true.

The life of Jesus is validated, not by His followers and opponents alone, but also by people who had absolutely no vested interest in Him. These people were the bystanders of history—some of whom actually were historians. Take for instance a man by the name of Flavius Josephus. He was a Jewish historian who mentioned Jesus Christ in his historical record. He also records some prominent historical figures surrounding Jesus. He mentions James the half brother of Jesus, and he also mentions the beheading of a man who promoted Jesus even before his fame spread throughout Palestine, John the Baptist.

Still other figures in history mention Jesus Christ and the fact that He was executed by crucifixion at the hands of Pontius Pilate. Pliny the Younger, Suetonius, and Cornelius Tacitus were historians and politicians, who were primarily interested in the development of Rome, not of Christianity, yet they found occasion to mention Jesus in their writings. Some of them even mentioned him in their correspondence with the emperor himself.[116]

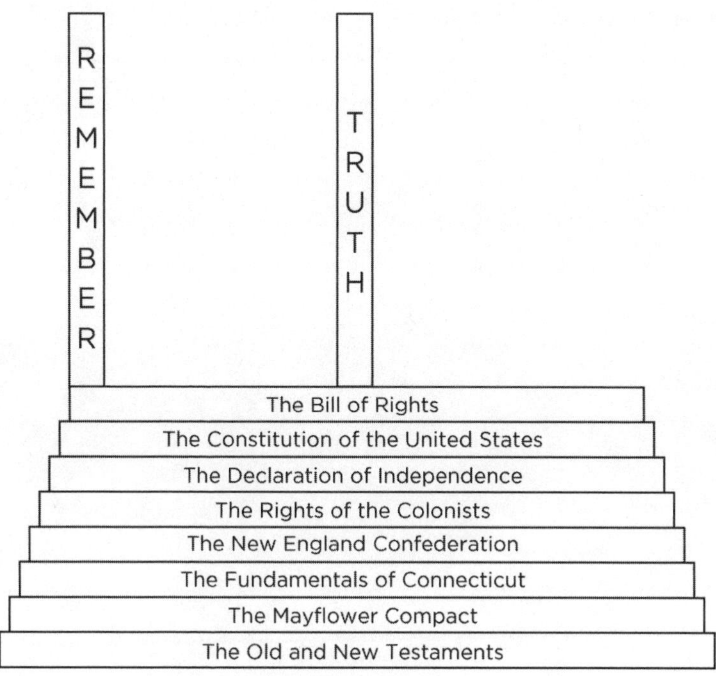

Figure 3 - DISCOVER THE TRUTH

THE THIRD LAW OF LIBERTY

Respect Humanity

CHAPTER NINE

Accepting Imperfection and Perfecting the Rejected

THE THIRD LAW OF LIBERTY IS TO RESPECT HUMANITY

Accepting Imperfection

Why were people so interested in Jesus? This question can be answered by exploring the third law of liberty, which is *respect.* People were interested in Jesus because He had a way of impacting an entire society, not to mention an entire empire and the rest of human history, by His authority. He did it in a way that none other has done before or after Him. He was not arrogant but humble. He was not cruel but kind.[117] He was not spiteful but loving. He did not use His power to persuade the masses to produce mob violence against the authorities but rather told them to support their governing authorities.[118] He used His own power, not to gain an advantage for Himself, but to benefit others.[119] He fought for those who could not fight for themselves.[120] He healed the helpless, gathered the outcasts, and restored the morally broken.[121] Through His actions and His words, He provided people with ways to overcome their fears.[122] In fact, many Christians to day claim they do not have the fears they knew before they met Him because of who He was and is.[123] His life was a true model showing how we should treat one another.

When a person faced Jesus, Jesus made that person face himself. Millions of people today attest to the fact that the words of Jesus provide people with the strength they need to face their worst fears. The courageous stand Jesus took as He faced death, followed by His resurrection, has equipped believers with the fearlessness that accompanies immortality.[124] The gift of Christianity is freedom from death and sin. When Christ conquered death, He destroyed the decaying element of humanity. The resurrection of Jesus empowers believers by His words and also by His spirit.

Therefore, Christ, the conqueror of death, is still on a conquest in the life of each individual believer. In this conquest, He equips people with the courage necessary for them to trust Him as He trusted his father.[125] Believers increase their faith as they trust Christ. Just as He submitted Himself to be crucified upon that cruel instrument in order to conquer death, we too have to take up the very instrument of our suffering and be crucified upon it in order for our worst fears to be conquered.[126] This act also restores a person to a position of self-respect. Individuals who live in fear and bondage produce societies that are bound. However, individuals who achieve freedom produce societies that are no longer bound.

The key for individuals according to the New Testament is that they have to believe Jesus is able to expunge the source of their fear. Once they believe He is able to do so, the source of their fear is obliterated.[127] He not only eliminated their fears, but He also taught them how to teach others this truth. This instruction was not some mystical transfer of power. It was and is a truth that originated, resonated, and depended upon Jesus.[128] A person who was freed from the chains of habitual bondage did not become the key of freedom for others. He did not become Jesus; he simply passed the key around to others. Jesus is the key. Believers were instructed by Jesus to share the key with others.[129]

The way that He taught them to do this was through love. Not just any love, but the deepest kind of love that exists. It is the kind of love that God displayed toward Adam and Eve even after they disobeyed Him.[130] The kind that causes onlookers to yearn as they take a step back in response to the display they had just witnessed. Jesus Christ not only displayed love and spread love, but He indeed is love. Without Jesus, there could not be love.[131]

Remember, God desired to commune with Adam and Eve as their Creator even after they disobeyed Him. So according to Genesis, He sacrificed an animal to cover their mistake, but they still died. The only cure for death was for God to sacrifice something more sacred than an animal. This sacrifice was His beloved son.[132] The Creator did something His creation could not do for itself. He demonstrated how much He longed to relate to human beings through the ultimate act of love. He set Himself up as the source of love and also as the standard of love. He made the most beautiful statements of love ever declared or demonstrated.

Therefore in the same way, regarding human relations, respecting other people is not simply a matter of accepting them for who they are. Respect has more depth than that. On the surface it seems very commendable to embrace people in spite of themselves. However, if the relationship has no more substance, it falls far short of the respect Jesus demonstrated.

An example might allow us to better understand that to accept a person without any expectation for improvement, does not really promote respect or freedom. A person who is one hundred pounds overweight as a result of being addicted to food (for whatever reason—depression, anxiety, or just because he likes food), is abusing his body by asking his heart to do twice as much work as it was designed to do. As a result of this abuse, this individual has demonstrated that he does not respect healthy eating habits and has neglected his well-being. He may not even like what he has become. This lack of respect for self may lead to even more abuse, such as the neglect of familial duties, personal hygiene, or even unhealthy isolation. Would not a true friend be one who attempts to help this person? Certainly to neglect this person is not to respect him. Respect in this case would be first of all to listen to this overweight friend in order to see if he wants to change. He has to have the desire to do so. A person knows when he or she possesses an undesirable quality. These same people may at times drop hints, actually cries for help, to family and friends. True respect in this case would be to answer these verbal or silent cries with assistance and accountability that would ensure success for the individual.

THE CONFRONTATION OF SELF-CONSUMMATION

What about the person who does not seem to drop any verbal cues for help? What about the person who does not care? When this happens, the most concentrated efforts to show respect are needed. Some may call this the dark side of respect. Mothers are notorious for this kind of respect. A mother who abhors smoking may have a child who ends up developing this unhealthy habit as an adult. However, out of concern for her child, she may plainly tell him she thinks smoking is a filthy habit. Even though her child has now matured and may no longer feel obligated to abide by the wishes of his mother, in her presence he may choose to put away the habit out of love and respect for her.

Some may argue that a mother's role allows her to attempt to dissuade a child from harmful behavior, but no one else has the same prerogative or position to correct a friend, let alone a stranger. Jesus however, felt that He did have the prerogative, especially when it concerned respect and humanity. He believed, practiced, and taught that people who cared for people needed to "judge with righteous judgment."[133]

There used to be a time, even in this country, when not only mothers would correct their own children but other older adults would correct them as well. It did not matter whether the adult knew the child or not. If a child or an adult was acting unruly or was misbehaving in public, someone would say something. Indeed, Abraham Lincoln administered the fervent challenge to "[l]et every American, every lover of liberty, every well wisher to his posterity, swear by the blood of the Revolution, never to violate in the least particular, the laws of the country; and never to tolerate their violation by others."[134]

The reason we do not hold others accountable to our laws today certainly is not because we have become more proper or refined. On the contrary, if anything, as a society, we have become more ignorant and crude.[135] Many people do not respect other human beings who are in need, or who need to be corrected, because we do not want the inconvenience of having to get involved. The fact is that many people feel uncomfortable confronting delinquents. Therefore, we have become a nation that does not love liberty but rather comfort. Comfort, apart from sacrifice, will eventually lead to bondage and ultimately to demise.

THE IMPRESSION OF EXPRESSION

Ideally, however, it would seem that out of respect, one human being should be willing to love a person enough to help him not only achieve freedom but also to preserve freedom for others. A person who is misbehaving in public may be robbing the freedom of the surrounding majority. In doing so he has demonstrated that he does not care for the peace or enjoyment of others but for self alone. When a public display of selfishness becomes obnoxious or injurious to the individual or even to others, it must be thwarted. Respect for humanity is preserved anytime undignified acts are extinguished.

Therefore, human beings have an obligation to speak out against harmful acts one person inflicts upon another or even upon himself. We should be morally outraged anytime someone degrades or debases the human image, whether the degradation is directed at self or others. Our license to say something has been granted by the mere fact that we too are human. All of humanity suffers within a society that allows the body of an individual to be mistreated because the overall image of humanity will be tarnished. Once humans no longer consider other humans as sacred, human life loses its value and ends up being viewed as common matter. When the individual human life is no longer seen as precious, it will lose its value within society. When human life loses value within society, all kinds of crude acts toward the body are condoned.

AN IMAGE TO UPHOLD

It is not very difficult to understand that the entire human image is in jeopardy when humans exploit themselves or others. Humans have a tendency to reflect what they see other humans doing. When a new technology splashes upon the social scene, (telephones, TV's, VCR's, answering machines, DVD's, cell phones, MP3's, personal computers, fax machines, PDAs, etc.,) human beings want to purchase it as soon as they find out that other humans have it.

The same rings true for fashion trends that envelope a society. Two decades ago very few men had tattoos or earrings, and if they did, with few exceptions, they only had a small number on their bodies. Today, it seems as though everyone at least considers the possibility of getting a tattoo. And why should we limit ourselves to just piercing the ear? We do not have to because there seems to be absolutely no sacred spot upon the human canvas immune from piercings. The new attitude many Americans express by boldly displaying tattoos and body piercings may be indicative of an increase in risqué behavior. Linda Marsa recently reported the following in the *Los Angeles Times*:

> Compared with their unadorned counterparts, adolescents and young adults with tattoos or body piercings were twice as likely to engage in sexual activity and use "gateway" drugs, such as marijuana, alcohol and cigarettes, the researchers found, and they were three times as likely to use hard drugs, such as Ecstasy, cocaine and methamphetamines. Males with tattoos were more likely to engage in violent behavior than those without tattoos, and females with body piercings were twice as likely to get into fights. Also, girls and young women with tattoos or body piercings had a higher incidence of eating disorders and thought more about suicide. And the younger both genders were when they got their body art, the more likely they were to be involved with gateway drugs. Since most adolescents with these adornments are older than 17, however, the tattoos and piercings could be a sign that young people are already in trouble. "It's probably not the first risky thing they've done," said Dr. Victoria Paterno, a pediatrician in Santa Monica, Calif. "They've already been drinking, and smoking cigarettes or marijuana. If you haven't picked up on other cues earlier, then you're probably pretty clueless as a parent."[136]

We now must consider another element of respect—that of conveying to others the character one possesses. This includes but is not limited to peace of mind, self control, and discipline. In no way does this person convey an attitude that says, "I am better than you." Certainly, there may be some people who correct others with that type of mindset. But true respect conveys an attitude that has more to do with the characteristics of wisdom and experience. True respect displays a desire to correct minor flaws today in order to avoid major malfunctions in the future.

Respect for the individual is more proactive than reactive. It is the type of attitude that may even communicate a familiarity with the current position of the cantankerous individual. As an older, more experienced individual reaches back to his own youthful experiences, he can promote respectability in a younger individual's life simply by intervening in such a way that encourages the youth not to make some of the same mistakes he himself made. This individual is truly empathizing with the younger individual by getting involved. He is not interfering to rob the youth of his freedom. Instead he is providing the individual with the opportunity to act more efficiently and waste less time.

MORTAL DANGER

If a society chooses to overlook disrespectful behavior toward humanity, it can lose a proper understanding of respect within one generation. If no one corrects the younger generation, then any semblance of respect will be lost when these youngsters become adults. What is not taught will be lost, much like the extinction of a species. Once the species becomes extinct, there is no way to resurrect the species. Professionals may continue to talk about and study the species, but it is of no benefit to the extinct species. It may benefit other species in that it raises awareness of what can happen when a species is over hunted or neglected, but it can never bring back what has been lost.

Many people have a difficult time trying to grasp how important respect is to freedom. Another practical example should give us a better understanding of how respect for human beings unfolds daily. If a person who had cancer was cured by a doctor's new treatment, it is likely that individual would refer others to this doctor with a passion so that they might be freed from the clutches of death. The cured would be singing the praises of this doctor and his healing treatment. On the other hand, if a doctor simply recognized that a patient had cancer without attempting to eradicate the problem, it is unlikely he would receive any referrals.

Simply recognizing, or even excusing, a behavioral problem does not help the person and is not considered a display of respect but rather negligence. Diagnosis of a problem needs to be met with an appropriate treatment in order for there to be a cure. In the same vein, it is important for us to recognize that respecting an individual involves more than accepting him without any expectation for improvement. Therefore, we must all recognize our responsibility to respect ourselves as well as others by remaining open to correction. This sociological attitude will not only promote universal freedom, but it will also promote respect as we acknowledge that within each human soul there is a desire to improve both physically, emotionally, intellectually, and spiritually.

PERFECTING THE REJECTED

Once again we must turn our attention to the one Person—Jesus—who demonstrated respect for the individual or the human image more than anyone else. It did not matter to Him the societal status from which a person came. He demonstrated that individuals deserved respect simply because they descended from the same source. Jesus taught that anyone of us could have found ourselves in similar circumstances had we been born in an impoverished, immoral, or crippling environment.[137] So He demonstrated that one could not respect another without compassion and love for all of humanity.

Jesus is the first person to teach and model what respecting others truly meant. He did this by teaching people they were obligated to love their neighbors. In addition to daily examples, He also did this through the use of parables. One of the most famous was "The Good Samaritan." This parable has a universal appeal not only because it is a good story but also because the original storyteller tells it. In this parable, Jesus made it clear that anyone we meet who has a genuine need is a neighbor simply because of our proximity to him or her.[138] This proximity is not simply a nearness of geographical position, but more importantly nearness in the sense that we are both human and, therefore, both created in the same image.

According to the Biblical account, the victim in the parable of the Good Samaritan did not speak. This did not matter to the Good Samaritan. He knew nothing of the individual's background. All he knew was that the individual needed some medical attention. The Good Samaritan is an excellent example of respect because he did for the victim not only what the victim could not do for himself but also what he would have wanted the victim to do for him had the situation been reversed.

Why did the Good Samaritan act? He understood this man to be his neighbor. Who is my neighbor? Anyone who reflects the image of God is my neighbor. Who reflects the image of God? All humans reflect the image of God. According to the Hebrew Scriptures, this lesson is the first and most important one God taught humans about humans.[139] Therefore, since God is the creator of humans, humans must first learn to love, honor, respect, and dignify the image of God. However, before humans can learn to love, honor, respect, and dignify the image of God, they must first learn to love, honor, respect, and treat all humans in his image with dignity. Why? Because there seems to be a direct correlation between the way people revere and respect other humans who are created in the image of God and the way humans revere and respect God.[140]

Herein lies the dilemma. We cannot love God until we learn to love humans, yet we are incapable of completely loving humans because we fail to love God. This was a vicious cycle that needed to be broken in order for the love of God to prevail. God deserved our love, yet we were incapable of loving Him completely because of the fall of humanity in the Garden of Eden. Therefore, even though we need to love people the way God loves people, we could not love people the way that God loves people until He came and showed us, as a human, just how much He loves people.[141]

He showed us love in His life, but He showed greater love through His death because he killed the very obstacle that prevented us from loving God completely. That obstacle was sin, which gave birth to death.[142] Death kept us from loving God completely because we were, comparatively speaking, lifeless beings. God is immortal, and we are mortal. An immortal being cannot holistically relate to a mortal being unless either the mortal being becomes immortal or the immortal being becomes mortal. The reason for this is simple. Relationships are based upon existence. The only thing that keeps a relationship alive is the life within the relationship. This life stems from living beings. When one of the life forms ceases to exist, that particular relationship also ceases. Although people attempt to keep the relationship alive by many means—visiting grave sites, reminiscing, or even going to the extreme of talking to the dead, eventually these feeble attempts will end.

Since immortality is greater than mortality, it is then possible for the immortal one to reduce Himself to mortality. According to Scripture, Jesus Christ existed prior to His birth to the Virgin Mary.[143] He existed with an unconditional, unquestionable immortality. When He became a man, however, He laid something of His person aside.[144] What was it that He gave up for a time? He gave up His unconditional immortality for the sentence of mortality. Jesus Himself said, "No one can take my life from me. I lay down my life voluntarily. For I have the right to lay it down when I want to and also the power to take it again. For my Father has given me this command."[145] For an immortal being to voluntarily set aside His immortality for a time to become mortal, He would have to become less in an existential sense but not less in a positional sense. In just this one statement, Jesus Christ acknowledged His mortality while at the same time asserting that He still maintained the power over His mortality. He had the position to exert the power over His existence and that is the key to individual freedom.

Before the incarnation, Jesus was above space and time; now He was subject to both. He did not lose His position in the godhead; His position was simply translated from the point of being glorified as God with God to glorifying God as man with God.[146] The immortality of Christ hung upon the condition of His undying obedience to the will of the Heavenly Father, even to His own hurt.[147] This is not to say that there was any possibility of failure, but rather it is a bold display of confidence that was guaranteed to succeed from the moment the Child was conceived. If He, as God turned human, could maintain ceaseless obedience to the Heavenly Father as human, He would have qualified all of humanity for an opportunity to become immortal.[148] Why? All that the Father needed to be satisfied was to have one Son who was in perfect communion with Him because that was the only condition placed upon humanity in the first place.[149]

From the moment the first man was created, he was a being whose existence depended upon undying obedience.[150] When the first man disobeyed the Immortal One (the Giver of Life), he severed the relationship by slitting his immortal wrists. However, if the true Son of God gave up His existence in heaven and shrank Himself to an existence on earth, He then would have the position to love God through humanity. If He could love God through humanity with the depth of love that He had as God, then He could heal the severed relationship. Every act of disobedience could be paid for by one act of perfect obedience.[151] But it had to be an act that would counteract the poison humanity had ingested. The first act of disobedience came as the result of the first man consuming the forbidden fruit—thus committing existential suicide. This was an act of the free will of man. God gave him the ability to obey or disobey. In order to remedy the results of that disobedient act, Jesus would have to release His free will to the will of the Heavenly Father. In doing so, He would be vulnerable to men who refused to submit their own will to the will of the Heavenly Father.

When Christ had His wrists pierced by the same hammering hands that He would that very day heal, He provided humanity with the vaccine for death. That vaccine was a concoction of His own blood—shed by a man who knew no sin suddenly becoming the embodiment of sin for the sake of humanity.[152] However, the only way to extract this vaccine was to puncture His body in order to allow this life-giving blood to flow. While it remained in His veins, He was a picturesque human, full of life. But when His blood was pounded out of His body, it was not subject to the lifeless breakdown of common human blood. On the contrary, it had unrivaled power that pursued and restored life at a rapacious speed. As His blood ran out into time and space, it restored mankind to his proper place. In fact, the Gospel of Matthew records that at the moment of Christ's death, "[t]he tombs were opened, and many bodies of the saints who had fallen asleep were raised; and coming out of the tombs after His resurrection they entered the holy city and appeared to many."[153]

This revitalization was unmatched and unrivaled by any other act in all of human history because for the first time a morally perfect man had died. This was not just any man. This was the very Son of God, the only man ever to be in perfect union with the Heavenly Father, and He died. The only man ever to completely satisfy the heavenly Father, and He died. He was untouched by sin in that He never had an evil thought, spoke an evil word, or took part in an evil act.[154] As a result, His life's blood was so efficacious that it did not cry like Abel's blood, it roared.[155] It consumed every sin ever committed. Sin had consumed life up until then, but now His perfect life would consume sin. Jesus Christ, the Son of God, had allowed the weight of every human sin ever committed to bury Him. The Heavenly Father stated in the Garden of Eden that the penalty for sin was death. This man, however, had never sinned but still died.[156] Every sin had been completely baptized into the blood of Christ; therefore, sin no longer reigned, Christ did, but He was dead.[157]

This was not something that a just God could ignore. Sin no longer existed; therefore, death had been conquered. How could death keep the Son of God in the grave if it was a penalty that no longer existed? The catalyst for death was sin; however, its reserves had been drowned in the life-giving blood of Christ. He had to restore the life of His Son because death was made extinct. Jesus Christ bore the weight of humanity; now the Father would bear the weight of His Son. The Father parted the sea of humanity and lifted the Son from beneath the pile. His hands figuratively brushed all of humanity in the process of calling forth the deity. As He reached down to earth to scoop up His Son in His arms, He embraced all of humanity. Because of the sacrifice of the Son, the Father rescued the Son, and by rescuing the Son, He restored humanity.[158] The Son of God had completely sacrificed Himself in order to rescue humans; this was in accordance with the Heavenly Father's will. Since the Son had completely given Himself to the Father's will, the Father honored the Son by accepting His sacrifice.[159] Now all that was left to be done was to demonstrate His satisfaction with the sacrifice by restoring His Son. Since the Son had taken upon Himself not only true and complete humanity, but also the sins of humanity, He was now one with humanity. The Father's complete acceptance of the Son would now also reunite humanity with the Father.[160] This complete acceptance included all that Christ's life and death had touched. Because the Son went to the depths of humanity, the Father raised the depths in order to restore His Son to the glory that He enjoyed before the foundation of the world.[161]

Since the Son died for humanity so that we might live, it would seem that humanity would want to live for the Son.[162] Jesus Christ taught us, as humans, how to love people the way God loves people. Therefore, He solved the dilemma. If people would only live for Jesus instead of themselves, then they would love like Jesus. This is not just some strident belief that seems to produce the most virtuous behavior. It is truth that can be validated by real human existence. Some modern philosophers, in an attempt to be honest using the most verifiable evidence, have abandoned the idea of God's existence but have recognized the benefits that belief in God produce. One of these philosophers by the name of Sir Julian Huxley, an atheist, declared that "somehow or other, against all that one might expect, man functions better if he acts as though God is there."[163] If we were able to observe consistently virtuous behavior, would we then not do well to consider the source of this behavior to be true?

God created man in His own image so that man would know how to respect the image of God. Once man learns to respect the image of God, he will be more prepared to properly respect the person of God. We were given the example of "God with us," (Immanuel)[164] so that we could be with Him.

We were given the example of Immanuel so that we could observe how a perfect human respects God. Jesus respected God by respecting the image of God. He did this by loving beings who were created in His image. We learn to respect God by embracing Immanuel. By embracing Immanuel, we are given the ability to love others the way God does. Therefore, we learn to respect God by practicing respect for other humans. Man is like a shadow that we can see. He is a shadow of the true God, but nonetheless a shadow. We cannot see God, but we can see His shadow. If we saw God in all of His completeness, we would be overwhelmed and, according to Scripture, would die.[165] So by His grace and for our own protection He gave us a glimpse of Himself through humanity. When we learn to love the entirety of humanity, we will be able to love God completely.

This, in no way, should be confused with the impersonal, pantheistic model of God mentioned in chapter seven. We are talking about a very personal God who is located and held together in triunity. This triunity is the icon for the way relationships should be conducted. There is a mutual adoration or respect within the Godhead that is unrivaled by any other relationship. Therefore, it has been theologically concluded from Scripture that God exists as the personalities in Trinity.

God as three persons in one should not be mistaken as some type of schizophrenic Modalism. God is not one person with three schizophrenic personalities. Rather, accurately understood, the Trinity in its historic sense is three persons who share one nature.[166] Not sharing in the sense that they pass the quality of Godness back and forth; but rather sharing in an uncompromising and equal manner. This should not even be understood as if the three persons are splitting up the deity as if it was a pie but rather that the three persons make up the deity.

God is completely, solely and universally God. He exists and always has existed in three distinct persons and one nature, that nature being God. The Godhead is equal because it is one. The only distinction that can be made is as it relates to the person's given roles within the relationship of the being of God. Therefore, the Godhead is respect and relationship in perfect and uncompromising unity.

It then makes perfect sense for the personal God to send His Son to earth to be born of a human as a human. Prior to the coming of God's Son, humanity still had not learned to love and respect the entirety of humanity, and therefore, had not truly learned to love and respect God. So what did God do? He sent His Son to earth to teach humanity how to truly love and respect humanity or the human image and concurrently to teach us how to truly love and respect God. He taught that God is pleased when we love and respect each other. We love God by loving each other.[167] This is not apart from recognizing or reverencing God, but it is the very act that allows us to remain qualified to commune with God at all.[168] That is why Jesus Christ taught us to forgive those who have trespassed against us. In fact, He seems to be teaching that we will be forgiven by God based upon how we have forgiven man.[169] Freedom cannot long exist in any relationship where there is no forgiveness.

The mistake of setting humanity up as God must not be made. We are not God. Humans are subservient to God. We are mere shadows; to take glory in our shadow apart from the source would be foolish and would extinguish who we are. A shadow is a byproduct of a body that passes in front of a light source. A light source is not the byproduct of a body that passes in front of a shadow. Therefore, without the light source and the body that passes in front of it, there would be no shadow. In the same way humanity would cease to exist without the Light.

Remember, humanity was incapable of loving humanity because of something that had misguided humanity, namely sin. If humanity is simply a shadow of God, and God is the source of light, then God's son would have to be the body that passed in front of the light to produce the shadow.[170] When sin came into the world it was as if something or someone else passed between the light and permanently altered or obscured the holistic human image.

Sin is what God is not.[171] Sin attempts to obscure God from humanity. There was something or someone that was sinister enough to think that it could still depend upon the source of the light to produce the shadow even if it stepped between the body and the shadow. Sin is to humanity what clouds are to plants.[172] Plants that need hours of direct sunlight and warmth to survive and flourish have a difficult time when there are extended periods of significant cloud coverage and drops in temperature.

In the same way, sin is the epitome of disrespect because it attempts to amputate the shadow from its source of life.[173] Its entire existence is based upon the idea that nothing is wrong, and therefore, nothing needs to be changed. Wrongs are not to be addressed but overlooked, and the only wrong that exists would be to call out or confront the sin of self or others.

Humanity needs the light in order to truly see itself for what it really is. The more the light is obscured the less humanity can be seen. Sin dehumanizes humanity. Sin degrades humanity. Sin attempts to consume human behavior through beastly behavior, and it ultimately desires to annihilate humanity until it is reduced to nothing more than Satan's feces.[174]

On the other hand, Scripture teaches that Jesus is the exact representation of God. Throughout the New Testament, He is referred to as the Son of God. He is the very image of God in the sense that He is equal to God the Father.[175] Therefore, He is God. He was not created but has always existed.

There came a time when He became human. Therefore, He took upon Himself the form of a human who was created in the image of God without diminishing His being. He did not always exist as human, but He did always exist as God. He could not have taken any other created form because, according to Scripture, there is no other creature that was created in the image of God.[176] God can become human without diminishing His deity. However, a human cannot become God because he was never God in the first place. God can become human because the human model was created in His very image. This is not to say that God was human in the first place. But it is to say that He placed His image upon humanity. Therefore, it could be said that humanity is compatible with God because God is the mold from which humanity was formed.

Jesus, though He was God, became human to demonstrate for humanity just how valuable humans are to God. He became human to demonstrate that humans are not God but rather created in the image of God. Humans had a beginning. Jesus always existed. Jesus, as human, demonstrated that the human duty is to submit to the image of the One who formed us. Since there never had been a human who perfectly submitted to God, Christ came as a human to demonstrate that submission could only consistently take place with divine assistance.[177]

Humans could not simply be told what to do, they had to be shown and then given the ability to satisfy God. This divine assistance came in the form of God giving all of Himself, not just a part, to humanity. According to the whole counsel of Scripture, Jesus is both completely God and completely man.[178] Just as God always existed, and man did not, so also, Jesus, being God, always existed, but not as man. He became a man at a point in time. That time came because man had rebelled against God.[179] Jesus came to honor and submit to God the Father as a human for the benefit of humanity.

Jesus did what He did to allow humanity to understand that He, indeed, was the body that stood in the light to produce our shadow.

A biblical understanding of the Trinity leaves one with the understanding that God is three persons and one nature; Jesus is the second person of the Trinity. The three persons of the Trinity share all of the attributes of the godhead. Therefore, even though Jesus is the body that stands in front of the light to produce the shadow of humanity, He also can legitimately refer to Himself as the "light of the world."[180] Furthermore, after He took on the form of a human through the virgin birth, He could also legitimately refer to Himself as a human. Hence, Jesus, in Scripture, is all in all.[181]

The point in disseminating this theology is that the Creator of man became a man to free man from the hijacking of humanity by sin.[182] One may ask why the Creator allowed it to be hijacked in the first place. This question alone may present further insight into the very nature of humanity or even the human design. Someone may ask this question out of frustration or resentment. Still others may ask this question cynically, concluding that there really is no creator. However, if the question of why God would allow humanity to be duped into sin in the first place is valid, then we have an opportunity, not only to understand more about the human design, but also about the designer.

God has enough confidence in Himself to create a being who truly has the freedom to choose or not to choose Him. Our choices do not affect or alter who He is, but they do affect who we are, for better or for worse. God knew how human existence would change based on our decisions. Here is where the mystery lies. He knew the outcome and yet was still in control of it either way because He cared enough to remain involved in the relationship.[183] He is, after all, the most personal being in existence.

Cynics may argue that He never relinquished His control of the human species in the first place. But this argument presupposes that a being as small as a human should have control in the same way as a being as large as the Creator. Man has freedom within the realm of humanity. He does not have control, nor can he control the realm of godliness. Therefore, a distinction must be made between freedom and control. One can still be free, within a given realm, without being in control of all realms. Man's duty was, and still is, to be in control of himself within the realm in which he has been placed so that he can enjoy the most freedom possible within that realm. Certainly, this is a reasonable expectation, for if he was unable to be in control of himself within his own realm, why should he be given any further responsibility in the realms of others?[184] Only madmen place uncontrollable individuals in positions of power. If one cannot control himself, then why should he be given the stewardship of others?

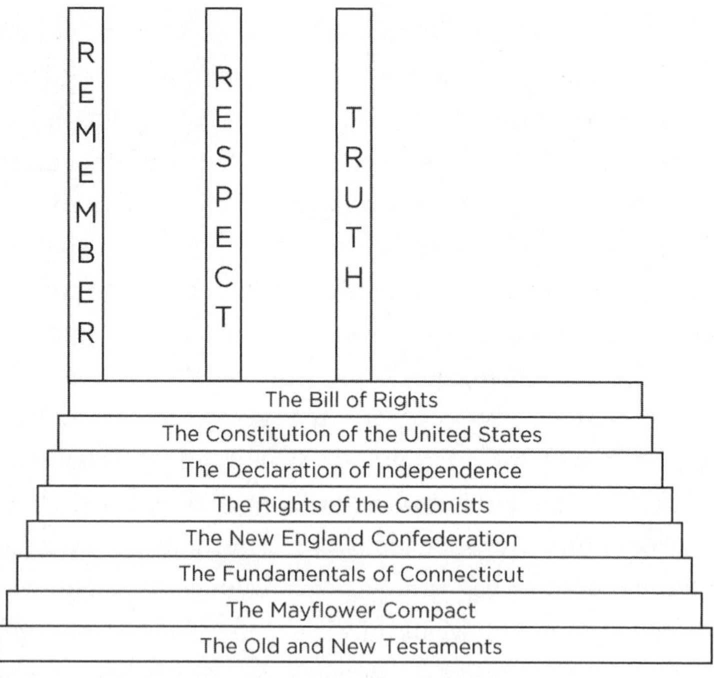

Figure 4 - RESPECT HUMANITY

THE FOURTH LAW OF LIBERTY

Control Yourself

CHAPTER TEN

Control Conceives Character

THE FOURTH LAW OF LIBERTY IS SELF-CONTROL

Self-control or Self-indulgence

Self-control is an indispensable commodity in order for a free society to exist. This fact makes self-control one of the greatest virtues an individual can possess. Self-control is also the fourth law of liberty. Not only does self-control benefit the individual by allowing him to pursue each day as a new adventure with few self-imposed hindrances, but it also benefits the society at large. Self-control could be defined as self-discipline or the ability to restrain oneself. Since the health of any society is dependent upon the citizens who make it up, then producing citizens who are capable of governing themselves becomes imperative.

Self-control, or self-restraint, is the fourth law of liberty because freedom, by its very nature, requires an individual to behave within certain parameters. Paradoxically, when an individual oversteps the boundaries of freedom, he is no longer free. Additionally, he prevents other individuals from being free. He has the freedom to jeopardize his own freedom, but once he does, he no longer enjoys freedom.

This situation can be compared to the ownership of land. A farmer may use and enjoy in many different ways the five hundred acres of land he possesses. He may allow his children, horses, dogs, or cattle to roam freely. However, the moment he, his children, or his animals step across the border, they are bound by the policies of someone else. He is restricted in the sense that his land is surrounded by his neighbors' land which does not belong to him.

Each landowner is responsible to maintain his own land. If he fails to manage his property, he could lose it due to natural or fiscal neglect. If he does not pay his mortgage, the bank can seize his property. If he fails to clean up debris on his property in a timely manner, he could run the risk of an unnecessary brush fire. If he loses his estate, it not only affects him, but also the members of his household. If he allows his property to become a junk yard or a garbage heap, this will not only affect his property value and the health of his family, it can also cause a drastic reduction in the value of his neighbor's holdings as well.

Furthermore, a lazy farmer who fails to maintain his land can actually damage another person's property. For instance, if he fails to check and maintain his fences, his cattle could escape. If his cattle escape, they could roam the land of unsuspecting neighbors. Cattle, as they are prone to do, relieve themselves whenever they feel the urge. In a cow pasture, that is understood and perfectly acceptable; however, a homeowner, especially if he has small children who place everything they see on the ground into their mouths would find this situation anything but acceptable. The neglect this farmer showed takes away the freedom of the unsuspecting family and places them in bondage.

Many people in our society fail to see the great responsibility that comes with freedom. They fail to recognize that the nature of their freedom has more to do with others than it does with themselves. They may enjoy the benefits of freedom, but free societies such as this one demand that their citizens take part in ensuring the freedom of others. Ensuring the freedom of others can only be accomplished through self-control. Sadly, an individual who fails to live within the boundaries of his freedom has a tendency to encroach upon the freedom of others. Oftentimes, these individuals do more harm to others than to themselves.

TAMING THE FLAME

Self-restraint and respect are intimately linked together. A person who has a proper understanding of self-restraint will have a better understanding of freedom. It is important to remember that true freedom is not getting to do whatever one wishes, whenever one wishes, however one wishes.

A person's desires cannot always be instantly gratified. Arguably, desires can be instantly gratified; however, if one ventures into the forbidden territory of instant gratification, there will be consequences. One consequence will be an undisciplined life enslaved by the chains of vice.

Another illustration will enable us to better see how self-indulgence can cripple the freedom of an individual and of the people around him. A young man who is attracted to the beauty of a young lady may find himself consumed with the desire to instantly take her into his arms and drink his fill of sexual pleasure. The more he gets to know her, however, the more he finds the attraction consists of other qualities about her he didn't initially see. She may have soft blonde hair, a cute smile, long legs, and eyes that beg him to pursue her. But he may also find that she is intelligent and articulate. He may be attracted all the more by her gracious demeanor. The more familiar he becomes with her, the more he will be intrigued, if she truly is all that he initially thought her to be. In fact, he will find that the initial lightning bolt that struck his eyes was a culmination of electricity radiating from the core of her being. Her beauty is obvious, but he better keep his passion from becoming inflamed too quickly, or he is going to get burned.

Physical attractions that can lead to the fulfillment of love are good desires, but they have to be tamed and properly placed. A man cannot take every woman that he desires. The fragility of freedom for both the young man and the young woman depend upon restraint or self-control. If the young man in the illustration succumbs to his desire to take the woman the moment the two of them are alone, then he would be guilty of rape. If he truly desires to get to know her more intimately, then he must be willing to invest the time necessary and allow her to consent to a relationship. If he is not willing to wait for her, then he has no business violating her. There are proper steps to winning a woman's hand, none forced. Even nature teaches us that the male-female relationship is and should be a beautiful dance.

To simply take what does not belong to oneself never produced freedom for anyone. The theft of innocence erodes the freedom of both the villain and the victim. The villain is held captive by the vice of his desires, habits, and addictions, and the victim becomes a prisoner of the villain's behavior. Everything gets tangled into his web of wishes. Unbridled lust extinguishes the blazing fire of liberty.

Clearly, freedom never grants the uncontrolled desires of some at the expense of defrauding others. To be sure, unrestrained desires can be trumpeted in the name of freedom, but that does not mean they are condoned by freedom.

ROYAL RESTRAINT

A classic example of self-control is found in Genesis chapter 39. It is a story that involves a promising young man named Joseph, the favorite son of Jacob, Isaac's son, Abraham's grandson. Joseph's brothers recognized their father's overt affection, and they despised their young brother for it. They became so jealous they decided to sell Joseph as a slave to a group of traveling merchants who carried him from Israel down to the land of Egypt. Over the course of time, he was eventually sold as a slave into the hands of a man by the name of Potiphar, one of Pharaoh's officers.

History records that Joseph was a good looking young man. He had an excellent physique and could efficiently manage every group of men from prisoners to planters, from servants to supervisors, and from officers to executives. His good looks, reputation, and ability to lead caught the attention of more than just his master Potiphar. One admirer, none other than his master's wife, stalked him.

In Egypt, sensuality was rampant, contributing to the madam's insatiable passion for a good-looking young man like Joseph. She pleaded with Joseph on a daily basis to sleep with her. She assumed that since Joseph was a young man and far from home, he would be more than willing to sleep with an experienced woman. But Joseph refused to violate the trust of his master and said, "How then can I do this great wickedness and sin against God?" (NKJV).[185] Joseph was exercising self-control by not fulfilling her demands. Potiphar's wife, on the other hand, had lost control. The sight of this man caused her to ignore any inhibitions she might have had. One day as he was passing through his master's house on his daily routine, she grabbed him by his clothing and commanded him to have sex with her.

Joseph, however, did not bend to her will. He fled, leaving his garment behind. Nevertheless, he was not rewarded by Potiphar for his temperance; on the contrary, he was falsely accused by the woman who now felt scorned. She produced Joseph's garment as evidence and built an argument against him saying he tried to rape her. Nothing could have been further from the truth.

Joseph exercised self-control when he was being seduced, and he maintained that composure even while he was being falsely accused. Unfortunately, Potiphar believed the accusation regardless of the fact that this kind of behavior was completely out of character for Joseph. His reward for such virtue was prison time.

Contrary to what most people understand today, Joseph was more free in prison than he would have been enslaved to an adulteress. Joseph was not driven by debauchery or controlled by corruption. Therefore, his life as a slave radiated more freedom than Potiphar's wife, though she commanded slaves.

This incredible young man was a model of self-control. Time and again, whether he was being forced into slavery by the family he loved or falsely accused by the female who desired him, he maintained his composure and excelled in every situation. Joseph stated his self-control was driven by his fear of the God of Israel. Scripture records that Joseph was a man who could be trusted with any man's goods. This trustworthiness created opportunities for Joseph. The Egyptians recognized that he had a quality lacking in their society—ability to control himself.

Joseph is an excellent example of a success story. But it would be very difficult for someone watching his life to see the success through the stress. He did not seem unnerved at any time, but the obstacles he faced while choosing to do the right thing would seem devastating to most other men. From Joseph's self-control grew incredible awareness of his surroundings; this awareness gave him singleness of purpose and the ability to manage difficult tasks. This ability, in turn, was recognized by his supervisors. His father, his master, his prison warden, and ultimately Pharaoh, himself, all recognized his capacity for trustworthiness in managing the most difficult situations. He could manage the most difficult situations because he had learned how to handle the most difficult relationships with men.

Joseph could be trusted with control over large tasks because he was faithful in controlling smaller tasks. Joseph could be trusted with power over many men because he could be trusted with power over one man, namely, himself. In every situation, Joseph unapologetically attributed this ability to his trust in God.

Those in authority can observe a person's ability to control himself as a means to determine the capacity that individual has of controlling others. A man is only prepared to govern others when he has demonstrated the ability to govern himself.

Joseph could be trusted with power, prestige, property, and people. This did not go without notice. The Bible records that Joseph was eventually given command over the Egyptian nation, second only to Pharaoh. In a real way, he was at last rewarded for his temperance. He could be trusted with power because he understood and obeyed authority—the highest of all.

Freedom could be defined as the ability to handle power responsibly. What then is power? Power is the authority to rule over people and property. Therefore, it is impossible to speak of power without mentioning these two components.

Joseph proved he could be trusted with property. He was put to the test when given autonomous authority over another man's possessions. The men who placed their possessions in his hands realized success because God blessed Joseph and made his work profitable. His parents profited; Potiphar profited; the prison warden profited; and even Pharaoh, the most powerful person in Egypt, profited.

Joseph could be trusted with people as well. Remember, power is the authority given to rule over property and people.

Joseph had been given the opportunity to interact with a broad band of people. In the process, he was exposed to a variety of ways in which people relate to one another and how they reward and punish one another. His early life had been a roller coaster of relationships. Joseph experienced the best and worst of almost every major institution: family, employment, and government. He experienced what it was like to be favored, first, and on top, and he was also subjected to the grueling experience of being nameless, unknown, and last.

His experience was such that the character and conduct of the people he served solidified his own character. This young man could not only be trusted with prestige (anyone can be trusted with that), but he could also be trusted with the authority to punish because he could empathize with those who unjustly suffered at the hands of others.[186] He understood what it was like to be misunderstood and falsely accused. Furthermore, Joseph had spent a significant amount of his young life in the presence of men who were paying their debt to society for their crimes. Instead of becoming hardened, Joseph allowed his fiery trials to purify his character and create balance within. These trials were the tools that God used to establish Joseph as a man who treated others the way he would want to be treated.

By the end of the tumultuous period in Joseph's life, he was literally sitting in one of the most prestigious seats in the entire world. A person could not have dreamed of achieving such a position because it was usually reserved for men who came from a long line of pharaonic royalty. Here he was, the advisor to the Pharaoh, himself. He had single-handedly spared this dynasty from ruin because of his solution to the coming world-wide famine. The God of Israel, who would later prove himself to be the one true God under the guiding hand of Moses, had his hand upon Joseph.

CONTROL CONCEIVES CHARACTER

The entire world came to Egypt because the young man Joseph not only had vision but character to match. A group of men of similar character who eventually made the difficult journey south from the land of Canaan were the very men who sold him into the hands of the nomadic merchants in the first place, his brothers. Since Joseph was in charge of the Egyptian food supply, no one made large purchases of grain without his supervision. When his brothers stood before him to buy grain, they did not know him, nor did he make himself known to them. The last time they had seen him, he was a teenager. Now he had become a man, experienced a change in culture, spoke a foreign language, had a new name, and achieved a position of authority. Joseph had the power to avenge himself for the suffering he had been subjected to by the hands of the men who now reached out to him in supplication. But instead of vengeance, Joseph released his power to forgive.

Herein lies the true meaning of freedom. Personal liberty allows the freedom of others to flourish as well. This type of liberty can only be achieved if the person in the position of power chooses forgiveness over revenge. The primary ingredient required to achieve this depth of freedom is self-control.

This component is so necessary because it is one of the only virtues that allows a victim to make decisions of unclouded judgment while dealing with his opponents.

Liberty cannot exist without this virtue of virtues; its survival depends upon forgiveness. When individuals understand the need to transcend their immediate desire for payback, then freedom can thrive. Joseph exercised this understanding, making choices that developed his character.

Character is the virtue of all other virtues, for without it, there can be no trust. Without trust, there can be no loyalty. Without loyalty, there can be no liberty. Trust cannot be purchased; it is something that must be tried and tested over and over in the lives of every person.

Whether Joseph's brothers realized it or not while they stood before him, he could be trusted with their lives even though he had more power in Egypt than anyone except Pharaoh. Conversely, when his brothers sold him into slavery, they betrayed him and lied to protect themselves because they lacked this quality. Joseph made choices as a young man that allowed the anchor of his character to become fastened to a rock that was strong enough to hold him steady even when the gale force winds of life blew. That rock was none other than the God of his life.

It was Joseph's faith in the God of Israel that allowed him to treat his brothers as individuals whom he loved rather than objects of hate. He was able to look beyond the sorry circumstances of his temporal bondage in order to see that God was using him to provide freedom for millions of people. As he stood on the other side of the storm, he could look back and see that the winds of adversity had blown him into a position of great advantage. His character enabled him to stay the course.

It was his trust in God that allowed him to keep making right choices. If he had abandoned his position prematurely, he would never have been allowed to see the masterpiece of God's plan. But he stayed faithful to the task at hand even when the consequences of his right choices seemed to mock him. This type of diligence freed him to look his brothers in the eyes and embrace them. Despite their selfish decision to sell him, he was able years later to say, "You intended to harm me, but God intended it all for good. He brought me to this position so I could save the lives of many people" (NLT).[187]

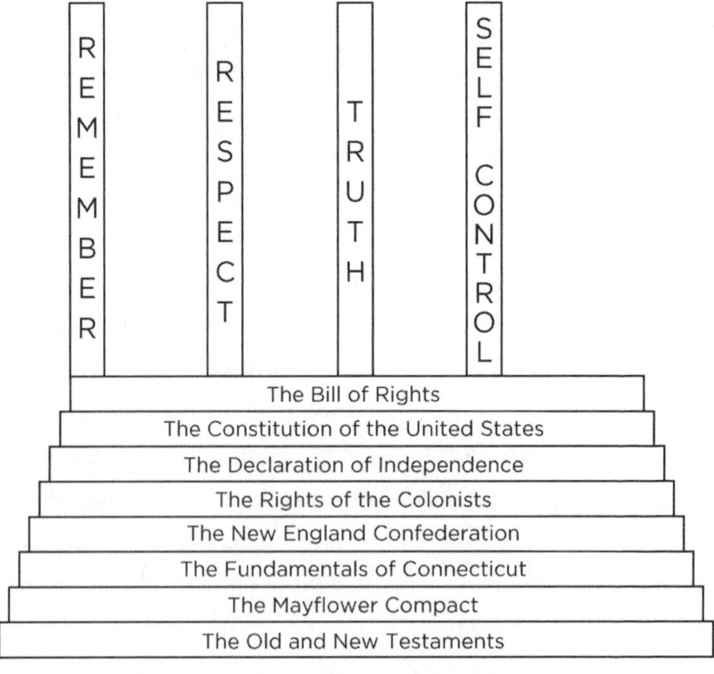

Figure 5 - CONTROL YOURSELF

THE FIFTH LAW OF LIBERTY

Protect and Serve Others

CHAPTER ELEVEN

MARRIAGE

THE LOVE-MAKING OF LIBERTY

THE FIFTH LAW OF LIBERTY IS TO PROTECT AND TO SERVE

IF THERE IS ONE WORD that concisely summarizes self-control it would be *protection*. As demonstrated in the life of Joseph, temperance acted as a shield, or protection, for himself as well as for others.

How can power be handled properly? The answer has to be found in the principle of protection. A man in a position of power should constantly re-evaluate circumstances and decide upon the action that would provide for the most protection for his people.

Control of self is the ultimate individual protection and naturally places a person in a position to protect others.

Self-control is the epitome of self-love. This is the purest kind of love because all other love stems from this love. This love is rooted in godliness and leads to contentment. Jesus Christ taught us to love ourselves, in fact he declared this type of love was the motivating factor in the proper treatment of others.[188] He taught us this by demonstrating not only how much he loved humanity as a whole but also how much he loved each individual. We must love ourselves because he first loved us.[189] We must properly love ourselves before we will ever be able to adequately love others. In order to properly understand how we should love ourselves, we must first understand how much God loves us. The major point of redemption, then, is to realize that the love of God not only consumes us but also compels us to follow his example of loving others.

It has been demonstrated repeatedly that when dealing with any of the five laws of liberty we must first discuss the self. The responsibility of protection is no different. If individuals do not protect themselves, they may not be around to protect others. Conversely, if an individual becomes consumed with a "survival-of-the-fittest" or a "king-of-the-hill" type of attitude, he will miss opportunities to protect others.

So how does one find the balance between the protection of self and the protection of others? According to the teachings of Jesus, there is no greater love than that a man would lay down his life for his friends; He also says that if people persecute you in one city flee to the next.[190] So which teaching is true? They both are. The truth is that there is a time to sacrifice for others, and there is a time to stand and fight for self. Sometimes it is only through fighting for self that one is available to fight for the safety of others. At the same time, many situations in life give rise to the responsibility of the individual to fight for the larger group of which he is a part. It then stands to reason that only while fighting for the preservation of the group can a man preserve self.

One example of protecting self for the safety of others can be found by examining the emergency procedures of a passenger jet. Standard safety procedures are reviewed for individual passengers before each flight. One such procedure has to do with a depressurized fuselage. The flight attendant explains that if this happens, the plane will automatically release oxygen masks from overhead. She continues by explaining that those passengers with small children should first place a mask over their own faces before attending to their children. If a parent spends too much time attending to the child before oxygenating himself, he can become unconscious. Not only would this neglect of self-protection put him in danger, but he would no longer be able to protect his child.

PROTECTING OTHERS INCREASES PERSONAL SAFETY

We are not doing anyone any favors by neglecting our own personal safety. However, to avoid jeopardizing our own personal safety, we must stand up and fight for the freedoms of others. We are not only to contend for those with whom we agree but also for those with whom we disagree. Ideologies should never become more valuable than the people who hold them. We should not hate a person for the ideas they hold; we should hate the ideas that hold the person. People are the ones who suffer when ideas are valued over people. There may come a time in our lives when we have to follow the example of Jesus by not only protecting religious and political allies but also religious and political opponents.

The past holds valuable lessons. One such concerns the value of human life, learned as a result of the Holocaust. After World War II, a German Protestant pastor by the name of Martin Niemoller described the consequences that resulted from his personal neglect of the people who suffered because of the ideas with which he disagreed:

> They came for the Communists, and I didn't object—For I wasn't a Communist; They came for the Socialists, and I didn't object—For I wasn't a Socialist; They came for the labor leaders, and I didn't object—For I wasn't a labor leader; They came for the Jews, and I didn't object—For I wasn't a Jew; They came for me—and there was no one left to object.[191]

FREEDOM FIGHTERS FOR THE FAMILY

Protection = Productivity

Accepting the responsibility of protection comes down to understanding the value of human life. After all, protecting something or someone is driven by that object or person's intrinsic worth. Humans are valuable because of our makeup. Therefore, the concept of protection depends upon seeing this value, poured into us as an investment. Once again, the concept of creation is invaluable. Creation of humanity, according to Scripture, is the idea that we are created in the image of God.[192] He poured Himself into us. Therefore, we all have intrinsic value. This idea is best understood through the relationship of the family.

In the beginning, God created the heavens and the earth. He designed these two spaces to work together and complement one another. In the same way, God created man and woman. He designated the institution of marriage as the epitome of commitment. In fact, the way that God created the first man was by "forming him out of the dust of the ground and breathing into his nostrils the breath of life; and man became a living soul." [193] Then after some period of time, God concluded that it was not good for man to be alone. Man was created as a being whose very purpose and meaning needed to be stimulated by the contact and cooperation of other human beings.

So the Almighty created woman. Many people know how He did this but never think of the significance of why He did what He did. God created Eve (the first woman) by casting Adam into a deep sleep. After the master anesthesiologist had prepared Adam for surgery, He removed one of his ribs. For years there have been skeptics who questioned the validity of such an account. Today, however, we understand that all of the DNA necessary to produce another human being was present within that one rib. Adam had a complete understanding of this concept as well, for after he had seen Eve he said, "This is now bone of my bones and flesh of my flesh; She shall be called Woman, because she was taken out of Man" (NKJV).[194]

God designed the man and woman to complement one another physically. Now, instead of reproduction requiring the division of an individual, God determined that offspring would be generated by the act of the male and female coming together. There would still be a sacrifice made on behalf of the participants, but it would now come from the overflow the love between the two produced. The power of this one love to reproduce depended upon the Creator of love. As the male and female depend upon the Creator of love, the two would now become one flesh.[195]

The first relationship was designed not only to be a complementation but also the ultimate in unification. One thing, however, we must not forget is that woman was taken out of man. This demonstrates God's ability to take from something, or somebody in this case, in order to produce someone else. It would stand to reason that the product or person produced would ever be indebted to the origin or source of the producer. Concurrently, the manufacturer would ever be responsible for the safety of the product. God designed man. Man was indebted to God. God gave of Himself in order to produce man. Therefore, God had a vested interest in protecting man, for in protecting man, he was, in a sense, protecting Himself or His investment.

In the same way, God designed woman. Woman was indebted to God and man. God gave of Himself and of the man in order to produce woman. Therefore, God and man had a vested interest in protecting woman, for in protecting woman they were, in a sense, protecting themselves.[196] God designated the man ultimately to take care of the incredible gift He had designed for him. He took woman from the rib of man—not just to have the information available in his DNA but also to remind the man that in protecting the woman, he was protecting his bone, and in protecting the woman, he was protecting his flesh. Eve was taken from the most protected location on the man's body. She was taken from an interlocked cage that protected the most vital organ in the man's body. She was taken from under the cleft of his arm.

Every time the man would place his left arm around the woman, he would be reminded of his role and duty to love and protect her the way that he loved and protected his own heart. He would remain with her all of his days because she was a part of him. God drew up the ultimate contract by designing Eve from Adam's rib. A word, a handshake, or a signature ratifies most contracts. This one, however, was conceived with more than ink and words; it was sanctioned with blood and the sacrifice of a bone. Therefore, through this one act, God instituted marriage as a lifetime connection between a man and a woman.

Together they would be one flesh. God designed Eve from the inside out so that Eve could communicate with Adam from the outside in. Adam would commune with his wife and know her with an intimacy unlike any other part of creation. He could become one with her by consummating the relationship. She had been taken out of his body, and he would now be received into hers. This reciprocation was a complementation. They could come together perfectly through sexual intercourse; they would stay together through intellectual intercourse and become one through spiritual intercourse. This is the only sexual relationship that was confirmed with God's approval.[197]

God's confirmation of this relationship can be seen in the fruit that is produced from the relationship. He put an entire system in place to respond to the sexual relationship. He designed the sperm of the man to be received by the egg of the woman. Once these two components came together within the uterus, all the genetic information necessary to reproduce a human being was united. Something wonderful, something amazing, something beautiful results from the ultimate expression of love. The beauty conceived within the woman is a replica of that which is outside the woman. The act of reproducing a man is the ultimate compliment that can be given to a man.

The husband is commanded to love the wife as he loves himself.[198] Reproduction only serves to clarify this truth. It is in loving the woman that the man truly has opportunity to see himself. When the little one who is a result of their union comes along, the man and the woman get to hold a part of themselves. What they gave as a part culminates in the whole of their reproduction. Through being wholly devoted to one another as man and wife, another human being gains life. After the child is born, the father may see his eyes in the child. He may see that the child has his mother's smile and her cute little dimples in his cheeks. This demonstrates a principle that God instituted through this relationship—the more the man and woman give of themselves, the more of themselves they will be given.

Marriage is a fascinating institution. It is also the most important institution known to man. It is the key to stability within any given society; therefore, it must be protected. Marriage should be taken seriously. When a male and a female are considering marriage, they ought to think long and hard about this lifetime commitment. Their conduct within this relationship, for good or for evil, will affect other people outside the relationship.

Abuse and Abandonment

Since marriage is the fountain of society's wellspring, it should not be seen as an experiment. It should not be seen as a novel idea. It certainly should not be altered. Marriage should be held in honor by all.[199] It is the most honorable institution in human existence. When marriage is disgraced, it contributes to the depravity of humanity. The institution of marriage should never be dishonored. Marriage is not for the faint of heart; individuals who take it lightly should be held liable for injury to the public.

Some ways marriage is debased today include abuse and abandonment. These two rogue characteristics do not produce freedom for anyone involved in the relationship. A man who abuses or abandons a family can be equated to a traitor who abuses or abandons his country. The man who treats his wife in this way does not see her as a person to whom he verbally committed his protection. He does not care about the dignity and equality of his spouse. If he does not care about protecting the one person who he vowed to "have and to hold," then it is unlikely he is going to value any individual at the expense of his own selfish desires. A man who abuses and abandons his own family has a flawed character and will not think twice about carrying that attitude into every other relationship, including those with other family members, friends, associates, and total strangers.[200]

A father acts as the shield of the family. There are times when a father may be incapable of completely fulfilling his familial duties. He could be stricken with a life threatening injury or disease. Worse yet, he may even be taken out of the way by death. Understandably, there is not much that can be done in these circumstances. But when a man volitionally chooses to harm or abandon those whom he is supposed to protect, he has demonstrated a disloyalty that amounts to treason.[201] This is especially the case when a man abandons a wife and his biological son or daughter. When a man abandons a son, he burns a negative image of fatherhood and freedom into the boy's mind.

Little boys, especially, need father figures in their lives. A father is the first male who challenges the little boy to be strong in courage, honorable in conduct, and mindful of people in authority. Most boys can think of all of the times during the course of a day that their fathers corrected them. "Take that look off your face." "You will not use that tone with your mother as long as I am around!" "What were you thinking?" These are just a few things that a boy may hear from his father.

In order for a boy to become the kind of man God intended, he needs to have a Godly man to imitate. Boys who never hear the daily challenge of their fathers to "stand up and act like a man" are likely to sit down and behave like little boys. A father may correct his son ten or more times in a day. Multiplied by a week, that figure may easily reach a hundred times. Over the course of a year, that figure reaches into the thousands. Granted, the fatherless may be corrected by his mother, but as he grows older, he recognizes that she lacks the physical strength to enforce her policies.

Because of the importance of the father-son relationship, a society is only as strong as its practical understanding and acceptance of the traditional family unit. Families are only as strong as the father of the family. It is true that there are some strong willed mothers. But it is also true that an entire family is a tremendous burden for one woman to carry. This load was intended to be shared by both parties responsible for bringing new life into the world. When a husband and father neglects his duties as the head of the home, the wife and children suffer. As a result, society also suffers.

In fact, someone has to pick up the slack for this sluggard, resulting in some type of church or governmental assistance. Consequently child support has become a critical legal issue. Oftentimes, it is difficult to track down an absent father and enforce the law when the man has neglected his duty to support his family.

Once again, we are confronted with a contradiction in our society. If freedom has no definitive boundaries, then why should the man be expected to support his neglected family? He should be able to stay in the home if he wants to stay or leave if he wants to leave. If freedom is what we make of it and not what it makes of us, then he should be under no obligation to the family that he took part in producing.

Additionally, the woman should have no qualms about his departure. Furthermore, if she wanted to leave him, the same unprincipled option should be available to her.

When this type of mentality is condoned within a society, the starkest depravity remains yet to be seen. For if a husband or a wife can abandon one another, then a mother and a father can abandon a son or a daughter. Both parents could leave the children simultaneously, without any type of repercussions. When the producers of offspring can abandon their children, the producers of offspring reduce society. All human life loses value when the commitment to the family by one or both parents is neglected.

Redefining and Declining

When the basic family unit is neglected, there are obvious consequences. Society then becomes burdened to resolve the ensuing problems. One problem that it must resolve is how to feed, clothe, and shelter the children who are left behind in the debris of neglect. These basic necessities require money. The solution, at least in our society, has come in the form of increased taxes. The individual taxpayer is tapped for some of his wealth. Instead of using his power to produce for his own family's future, he is now asked to make up for the neglect of someone else. This decline in earnings results in a deficit for the responsible family and actually contributes to the overall deficit of the country. When producers are excused of their duty to provide, without any type of ongoing repercussions, they become reducers.

When society does not enforce its laws to hold negligent heads of households responsible, then it must deal with the deficit by coming up with some other solutions. When the government allows a man to leave his family by running off with another woman or to neglect his responsibility for the children he brought into the world, this government is tampering with the basic family unit. Negligence on the part of the father should reap consequences, not breed more negligence. The government is behaving just like the irresponsible father by not forcing him to take responsibility for his actions. Any time an institution does not enforce the law, it unfortunately, endorses the lawless. In this case, by endorsing the behavior of the lawless, it is tampering with the basic family unit.

This tampering has led this society to a point when there are many different and acceptable ways in which a family can be described. In redefining the traditional family, the government has endorsed negligent parents and, in many respects, become a negligent parent itself. The government will never be able to deal as kindly with its children as the natural parents. Sure, the government may have the money, but it does not have the time. Secondly, it does not have the people, at least not the best people or person for the job. No one can ever adequately replace mommy and daddy.

Our society has developed a habit of excusing negligence for fear of moral reprisal. We claim to be free and have come to understand freedom to mean freedom from the responsibility to care for and protect our own. Our government has encouraged this attitude by becoming an industrial provider for those who are negligent instead of behaving as the guardian of responsibility. This provider role seems to be more benevolent at the outset. However, this perception has little to do with reality. We adopt the mindset that it is better to treat a problem than to cure it. Our minds have been saturated with the idea that to attack the problem is less tolerable than to excuse it. The consequence we face as a result of this ideology is to produce more programs.

Government programs that fail have only splintered into more programs.[202] We have become a society that reacts to familial issues rather than takes proactive measures. This approach has become the impossible mission. However, the problem can be solved by dealing with the primary issue of the responsibility that a parent has to stay with and protect his own children. Every time the governing authorities fail to hold a negligent parent responsible for his children, it breeds irresponsibility. The more that irresponsibility is bred, the less valuable its citizens become and the more valuable the central government becomes. When governments allow their citizens to behave irresponsibly, when they do not throw that responsibility back upon the individual, but rather assume his responsibility, they take over a role that does not belong to them.

The family suffers when government condones irresponsible behavior by taking over territory once expected to be cared for and cultivated by the family. This expanded territory produces a larger government, splintered families, and reduced family size. As the government grows, it gains more control, becoming authoritative in other areas as well. These other areas are not limited to controlling irresponsible individuals. On the contrary, these additional areas encroach upon the freedoms of responsible individuals as well.

The solution to this predicament is simply to address the problem instead of reacting to it. Accomplishing this is as simple as teaching young people that having children is reserved for the institution of marriage.[203] We must teach children and young adults that "it is good for a man not to touch a woman"[204] outside of marriage. Children are expected to control themselves in so many other areas, why not this one? The fact that there are teens and young adults in this country who have maintained their virginity up until their wedding day is proof that self-control not only can be exercised, it must be exercised.

Any deviation from traditional marriage must be seen as a direct attack upon freedom at large. A young man who impregnates a young woman before marriage should be, by law, expected to marry her.[205] This idea is punitive but also preventative. A young man who realizes the weight of his action is less likely to follow through with a passing desire. This concept will not prevent premarital relationships any more than capital punishment prevents murder. But it would definitely cause a young man to think twice about what he does and with whom. This may be just the right remedy to discourage the birth of children out of wedlock.

Furthermore, men and women who have sex outside of marriage should be expected to provide for the children they bring into this society. Even the New Testament teaches that "if anyone does not provide for his own, and especially for those of his household, he has denied the faith and is worse than an infidel" (NKJV).[206] Requiring parents to take care of their children would transform this situation from an impossible task for the government into a manageable task for individual families. It would also free the government to provide other benefits for society.

In order to protect the freedom of our society, we have to protect the existence of the family. The only way protection of the family can be accomplished is to have a strict definition of marriage. If marriage is the epitome of commitment in any given society, then any society is only going to be as strong as the value it places upon marriage. If marriage is weakened, then society becomes burdened with the cumbersome and impossible task of picking up the pieces where the irresponsible couple left off. In order for our society to guard against attacks upon individual liberties, we must view the institution of marriage with honor once again.[207] This means the idea of casual sex must end. The marriage bed must be guarded in a way that punishes those who stray.

When a man cheats on his wife, he must be punished because he has also cheated society. His infidelity has to be seen as one of the greatest attacks upon freedom because he has taken part in a disloyal practice that knows no equal. The greatest trust in existence is the trust that exists between a husband and a wife, and to violate this trust is to breed distrust and disloyalty in a society. America's freedom depends upon and is protected by loyalty, strong virtues, and trust.

Any time a woman consensually behaves in an impure manner prior to marriage and is found out, she needs to wed the man she was involved with in order to preserve freedom. For those who cry out that this idea is archaic or unreasonable, they simply need to observe the last fifty years in our society, namely that "free love"—the mantra of the 60's—is not free. On the contrary, free love has a price, and the price that is paid is as real as the cash that is exchanged between a man and a prostitute. In this case, society is not only the one getting abused but also the one having to fork out the cash for someone else's sexual addiction. Even a prostitute is wise enough to see the folly in such an exchange. She does not pay people to have sex with her.

Any type of sexual favors performed outside of the matrimonial bonds is a threat to a free society. Freedom depends upon the sound institution of marriage. Marriage, and what defines it, must be guarded at all costs. Irresponsible passion outside of marriage, whether it is pre-marital or extra-marital, leads to the denigration of liberty in the society at large. Consequently, couples who cannot control their passion should be encouraged to marry, limiting the act of intercourse to the institution of marriage and thus preventing it from spilling over and morphing into all kinds of counterfeits and perversions. Furthermore, this approach would save our society from having to spend so much time legitimizing something that is illegitimate. Society would not have to redefine marriage with thirty different scenarios that actually eradicate true marriage.

Marriage must remain between a man and a woman. Anything else is a feeble attempt to imitate marriage and is a direct attack upon the family which, in turn, is also an attack upon freedom. Consider the idea of homosexuality, for instance. Homosexual couples argue that they can remain monogamous and, therefore, have just as much right to be recognized as a married couple as heterosexuals. The problem with such a union is that it diminishes the role of one gender. If two men want to get married, they are communicating to the world that females are unnecessary, whether they intend that or not. This mentality, if allowed to run its course, could cause the role of the wife and mother to become extinct.

If two women want to get married, they are communicating to the world that men are unnecessary, whether they want to or not. This mentality, if allowed to run its course, could cause the role of the husband and father to become extinct. If one argues that each partner in a same-sex marriage would play a distinct role (mother and father) then they have just born witness to the authenticity of traditional heterosexual marriage. Furthermore, this argument has absolutely no objective standard behind it to establish the roles within the relationship. At least with traditional marriage, nature allows everyone to clearly see which person is the mother and which is the father, eliminating gender confusion for the children who may be involved.

Children need definitive and concrete examples of orderliness. Homosexuality is an avalanche of disorder. In marriage, a child can understand that mommy is a girl and daddy is a man. In homosexuality, a child, no matter how much he is educated, will have difficulty understanding the perverted abstract that daddy is a man and that the other daddy is a man. Mommy is non-existent. The child of such a scenario will definitely have a skewed view of the most basic human relationships.

Probably the most detrimental result of this union is the blurring of the lines of human sexuality in the mind of the child. If sexual intercourse is not limited to a lifetime, monogamous relationship between a man and a woman within the bonds of marriage, then sexual intercourse has no boundaries. No amount of education will convince a child otherwise. One cannot tell a child who is blossoming into a teenager that at one time sexual intercourse was viewed as limited but now it is legitimate for two grown men or two grown women to engage sexually with one another.

If our society condones the practice of homosexuality for this generation, then it will have to condone the practice of pedophilia in the next. If sex is not limited to traditional marriage, then there is no possible way to authoritatively eliminate any other type of intercourse. Unfortunately, we do not have to wait until the next generation because some people in our society, such as the North American Man/Boy Love

Association (NAMBLA) have already begun to exploit the hypocrisy of generational morality.[208] Even if people argue that not all homosexuals are interested in sexually exploiting children, they would still have to recognize that when we, as a society, validate sex outside of true marriage, we run the risk of exploiting the most innocent individuals in our society. They would still have to recognize that there are indeed people who do want to exploit children, and as a result of their culturally certified orientation, they certainly would not be able to deny their rights to someone else who has a depraved taste for little children.

When traditional marriage is not protected, other unions will be promoted. When other unions are promoted and accepted, then eventually, any consensually conceived orientation would have to be accepted as well. The children are those who will suffer the most. It does not take much to manipulate the desires of a child, especially, when that becomes the all-consuming desire of a pedophile. Adults who desire sexual relations with children become masters of persuasion. If sex outside of traditional marriage is condoned, then there really are no sexual restrictions. When the standard diminishes, there can be no replacement. Outside of marriage, a homosexual couple living together has just as much validity as a heterosexual couple living together. A bi-sexual triumvirate has just as much validity as the homosexual couple. And finally, a pedophile living with a consenting child has just as much validity as the bi-sexuals.

We must exercise the responsibility that we have to protect traditional marriage; not to do so is treasonous. When human sexuality is overemphasized, the value of the family is de-emphasized. When the family loses its value, humanity loses its value. Humans suffer when the basic institution that was designed for our growth and development becomes extinct. An overemphasis upon human sexuality is nothing more than an overemphasis upon individual liberties. The selfish desires of the individual are paid with the sacrifice of the entire family unit. Humans become objects to be possessed when they are simply reduced to objects of sex.

This fact is also why pornography is so dangerous to a society. Pornography promotes the idea that humans are nothing more than objects of sex. The emphasis is placed upon the human as an object to be possessed. This practice has a tendency to dehumanize humans. By increasing their sexual value, their overall value diminishes in every other area.

A danger arises in a society that overemphasizes sexual relationships—humans become nothing more than material to be used and discarded. The humans who are exploited the most are the ones who can defend themselves the least. Our society has proven statistically that since the onset of the legalization of pornography, sexual assaults against women and children have increased dramatically.[209] Furthermore, our authorities have experienced the difficulties of policing an industry that is dedicated to exploiting children. Once again, we run into some serious ethical issues when we try to legalize pornography for certain ages while punishing the industry for its use of younger individuals.

Another danger that plagues a society whose sexual ideologies have run amuck, is an increase in casual pregnancies. Instead of conceiving children and bringing them into traditional homes where they will be nurtured and cared for by their biological parents, they are born into a world without a committed father and, in some cases, without a committed mother, as well. A society that teaches the permissibility of promiscuity should not only expect this result but should also expect it with frequency.

Our society has come to defend its sexual ideas to the point of attacking the family. We have invented all kinds of technology in order to protect our sexual obsession. Some of these devices are proactive and some are reactive. These technologies include birth control, morning after pills, and abortion, among others.

CHAPTER TWELVE

MOTHERHOOD

THE LAST LINE OF LIBERTY

THE PILL

Birth control comes in the form of pills and prophylactics. As our society preaches the message of "safe sex," it does so amidst a newfound morality. According to today's logic, people can enjoy all of the sex they want as long as they are responsible in doing so. Men need to wear condoms, and women need to be on birth control. Birth control advocates expect any woman of childbearing years to be "on the pill." We have to ask ourselves, from where has this mentality risen? Why are we so paranoid about pregnancy? The answer stems from society's need to protect the exercise of personal pleasure from any of the natural side effects.

This is not an argument to condemn all forms of birth control. Even Jesus referred to eunuchs "who were that way from birth and some who were made eunuchs by others, and some who became eunuchs for the sake of the kingdom of heaven."[210] A eunuch is a first century reference to a man who was subjected to castration. Admittedly, it can also refer to a commitment that he made to a lifetime of celibacy. Arguably, this can be viewed as a primitive form of birth control.

Married couples use birth control to plan how many children they will have. Predictably, the size of the family is shrinking. [211] Our grandparents usually came from much larger families than what we see today in American society. Some arguments in favor of smaller families have to do with income. "A couple who cannot adequately clothe and comfort a child should not bring a child into the world" is a common statement made about procreation. "Better to procrastinate than to procreate" could be a possible slogan for married couples today. What is all of the fuss about? Why are we so anxious about the economy of the family? Not only did our grandparents have more children, but, in most cases, they did so with less money. Some might argue that the cost of living has increased. This may be true, but we also have larger homes and more numerous gadgets for comfort and ease than most of our grandparents did. Our society places more of an emphasis upon luxury and leisure than did our grandparents.

Is income supposed to be the driving force behind how many children a family should have? Or are we simply guarding the contraception industry that exploits the fears associated with childrearing?

Married couples are not the only group using birth control. Its use is encouraged and various forms are distributed to unmarried singles, especially adolescents. Why is this the case?

What kind of message is sent to a teenager who is being told by an adult, "You are going to have sex before marriage, and when that time comes, do it responsibly"? Do we handicap the young in any way when we provide means for them to enjoy sexual pleasure without any type of long-term commitment or responsibility?

We live in a society obsessed with controlling productivity. We try to control production on assembly lines, in the stock market, and in the womb. Does this obsession encourage more responsibility, or more negligence? Does this mentality communicate that we value pleasure over productivity? And if it does, maybe that reveals an even larger epidemic in our society. Freedom depends upon humans being allowed to grow, develop, and flourish. That can never happen if our existence is threatened in the first place.

A look into history can again allow us to see more clearly today. In the latter part of the nineteenth century, a battle raged in America over the concept of birth control. A lady named Margaret Sanger[212] made no qualms about promoting the ideas she believed in so strongly. She is remembered for her bout with the Comstock Laws, which were laws banning many types of birth control. She also played a major role in an organization in New York dedicated to global population control.

Initially the idea of controlling the population seems to be a good one, especially in densely populated cities, during times of economic collapse. The argument is driven by legitimate fears of shortages of land and food supplies. However, other reasons contend that every child should be a wanted child and have nothing to do with the scarcity of food or land. As one probes more deeply into the issue, he soon discovers a principle demonstrated throughout history—what cannot be prevented must be remedied. Even a brief glance at the origins of birth control allows an individual to see the correlation between controlling birth and the elimination of it.

If there is no inherent value in giving birth to a child, if all we are dealing with in the make up of humanity is matter, then it does not matter what we do with this matter. On the other hand, if the family was created by God to be the highest institution on this planet, then we should be very cautious about how we approach controlling the womb.

THE HERB YIELDING SEED

In the Hebrew Scriptures, God taught that not only humans outside of the womb have value but also humans inside of the womb do. One of His first commands to Adam and Eve was to be "fruitful and multiply."[213] He did not say, "Take care that you do not forget to take your pill." Even a brief glance at creation demonstrates how concerned God is with reproduction. In the first two chapters of Genesis, the writer mentions more than once "the herb yielding seed." Just by slicing a tomato open, one can observe hundreds of seeds that are produced from that one piece of fruit on one plant that sprouted from the germination of one seed of the multitudes from another plant.

In the same way, as humans unite to reproduce, God designed the man to be able to cast hundreds of thousands of seeds into the fertile soil of his wife. She carries one egg a month that has the possibility of being fertilized. The question is, should this be prevented? If a society values careers, convenience, and control, then the answer is, "Yes, it should be prevented." But according to the opening chapters of Genesis, we are not directed toward career advancement and convenience. In fact, because of careers, convenience, and controlling conception, we are not producing any fruit; instead of multiplying, we are remaining neutral. This would have been a foreign concept to the Hebrew people, for in their culture, God, through the Scriptures, taught them to not only value human conception but also to value the building blocks that make conception possible.[214]

THE EXTORTION OF ABORTION

The dignified young woman is the last defense for the unborn. Dr. James Dobson in his book, *Bringing Up Girls*, displays an excellent quote concerning feminine dignity from John Adams, the second president of the United States.

> From all that I had read of History of Government, of human life, and manners, I [have] drawn this conclusion, that the manners of women [are] the most infallible Barometer, to ascertain the degree of Morality and Virtue in a Nation. All that I have since read and all the observation I have made in different Nations, have confirmed me in this opinion. The Manners of Women, are the surest Criterion by which to determine whether a Republican Government is practicable, in a Nation or not. The Jews, the Greeks, the Romans, the Swiss, the Dutch, all lost their public Spirit, their Republican principles and habits, and their Republican Forms of Government when they lost the Modesty and Domestic Virtues of their women....

> The foundations of national Morality must be laid in private Families. In vain are Schools, Academies and universities instituted if loose Principles and licentious habits are impressed upon Children in their earliest years. The Mothers are the earliest and most important Instructors of youth.[215]

According to John Adams, as the women go, so goes the culture. Some, to be sure, might assert that this is untrue, men drive the culture, to which he may respond, yes but women steer the men. This, "barometer," of culture can be traced all the way back to the Garden of Eden.[216]

If a woman can neglect her self-worth by engaging in promiscuous acts, she has simultaneously reduced the worth of the unborn. Even abortion advocates promote the idea that the unborn is a part of the woman's body. If she devalues her body, what makes anyone think she is going to value the child growing within her body? This is the effect of porn and prostitution. These acts do not affect the participants only; they affect all women. When a society condones pornography and prostitution, many men come to view all women as whores. Most women view most men as only after one thing. As a result women feel as though they are held captive. A man can have his way with a woman and leave without any threat of being inconvenienced in the future. A woman, on the other hand, could be faced with the prospect of pregnancy. Her only solution is to do away with any unwanted consequences.

The child produced from promiscuity always suffers. When a man and a woman view sex as casual, anything that results can be casually dismissed. Sex must be reserved for marriage, and marriage must be held in honor. When it is not, humans may feel more sexual freedom, but the result is a reduction in the value of humans. When sex becomes casual, human life becomes convenient. Casual couples begin to think of the child who may result in terms of convenience. "A child is not convenient for me at this time." The child is spoken of in terms of a choice. It is optional. That is exactly what happens in a casual society.

This leaves our society with three options—chastity, child, or choice. Chastity requires an individual to exercise self-control. A person who practices chastity is denying himself immediate pleasure. This control of self translates into the protection of others. No one has ever ended up pregnant by remaining chaste, with the exception of the Virgin Mary. So in a chaste environment, no one ends up with an unplanned pregnancy, and no child is born out of wedlock. If a couple did fall to the temptation of having sex prematurely, which has happened throughout the course of human history, they should follow through with what they began—they acted as if they were married, so they should get married, have, and raise the child.[217]

The last option is to leave pregnancy open to choice. This action is in dark contrast to the lackadaisical one that brings women to this point. This decision is a cold response to the warm embrace experienced during intercourse. Choice allows one human to determine the value and existence of another human. Only one step stands between the child and death. Choice allows for the child's life to be reduced and erased. He can be annihilated on a whim.

A mother's womb has been designed to be a safe, warm haven from the outside world. The child is insulated from all of the worries of daily living. He simply has to enjoy the cradle of the perfectly tepid bath that has been drawn for him.

This is the safest place on earth for such a tiny baby. However, if a child finds himself growing inside a woman concerned primarily with convenience, and she feels him to be inconvenient, then the baby is in the most dangerous environment imaginable.

Abortion is the climax of birth control. When this peak is reached, it does not result in deep throaty moans of indescribable pleasure such as accompanied the conception of this little life; on the contrary, the climactic result of abortion results in the silent screams of an indefensible pain coming from a tiny mouth, located in the womb of a woman abandoning her role as a mother. That is what abortion does. It does not just snuff out the fragile flame of life, it kills motherhood. This ideology has stolen from women the very identity that distinguishes them from men.

A woman was designed by God to embody femininity unrivaled by any other creature. According to Scripture, the way that a man preserves his identity is by loving his wife.[218] That is a prohibition against loving other women. Men are required to focus passionately upon their wives.[219] The way that a woman preserves her identity is through childbearing.[220] Granted, not every woman can have a child. But those who can should embrace and revel in their God-given ability.

The home front is the last major battlefield to preserve freedom. How do we, as a nation, preserve the family? It has to begin with young men and women. It is no secret that men have always valued the sexual treasure that a woman possesses. Instead of allowing anyone and everyone to partake of her treasure, a woman needs to use the sexual aura that she possesses to seduce the man of her dreams. She should guard the beauty of her garden[221] so that she is able to say to the man she desires to marry that she has never been with another man. Her value infinitely increases, especially if she is able to look her man in the eye and say, "Though I have longed to be touched, I saved my treasure for you to explore." By this she means he will be the first man ever to see her naked, that no man has yet held her supple breasts in his warm hands, no man has yet kissed her virgin lips.

A woman who is able to say such things exemplifies an inner beauty that all men desire.[222] She also places herself in a position to barter with her treasure. She is fine and untouched and, therefore, is more valuable than those women who have allowed themselves to be driven by the "wild child" or the "bad boy." She is a true princess, her inner worth evidenced and guarded by her outward conduct. Once more, Dr. James Dobson has an entire chapter dedicated to the subject of the "princess movement." In this revealing chapter entitled, *The Obsession With Beauty,* he quotes from various everyday women who desire to be cherished for who they are, respected for their intelligence and honored as "equally valuable contributors to society."[223] A beautiful virgin can name her price; she is in control. Instead of having to deal with the consequences of promiscuity, she guards the treasure hidden within. This treasure will only be opened for the man who pledges allegiance to her by making a lifetime commitment marked by a seal he places on her finger. Once the engagement period is over and the vows are said, they can enjoy a rapturous and intoxicating relationship, and one day another life may spring forth as a result. Instead of detracting from the relationship, this new life becomes a cause for celebration.

Abortion is the worst form of self-hatred because it leads to self-mutilation. A baby who is produced from a relationship is the by-product of the material makeup of the relationship. To destroy the child is to destroy a part of the participants. A mother who allows an abortionist to willfully enter her womb and rip the baby from her is allowing him to kill a part of herself. She is also killing freedom because she is neglecting one of the most basic covenants known to mankind—motherhood. It is stronger than any other relationship known to man. No contracts have to be signed, no verbal agreements; a mother-to-be simply gets to experience the creative process working within her womb. A connection exists between mother and child that starts with conception and grows throughout pregnancy. The bond with the baby will continue to grow long after the child is born.

When people approach marriage as total commitment, then their families are based upon total commitment. Wives are treated with undying love, and husbands are treated with undying respect. The children benefit from this relationship because they, too, are valued as the offspring of a committed relationship. Everyone in the family is valued as a vital part of the whole. This type of family enjoys a radiant loyalty unrivaled by any other organization.

However, when people approach marriage as partial commitment, then the true concept of marriage within a society begins to die. Families are produced but may be broken or extinguished. Women are mistreated, and the very image of man is disrespected. The children suffer from this ill-treatment the most because they are valued no more than the relationship within which they are conceived. Maybe in this idea lies the most sobering revelation of all—that a relationship is only as valuable as what it produces. When we abandon or kill the offspring of a relationship, that is a demonstration of how little we value the relationship because we are killing the very life produced by the relationship.

ARMED AND DANGEROUS

Our ability to think clearly as a society is handicapped when we mistreat our offspring. This mistreatment often manifests itself in the unthinkable. We begin to rationalize and justify unethical actions that are driven by invalid arguments and selfish desires. We have been led to believe that abortion should be legal because of flawed relationships, economic and personal instability, convenience, and fear. Fear is the fuel of insecurity. We make pre-emptive strikes upon the womb based upon partial information. Instead of solving a problem, we think that by killing an unborn child, by playing the role of God, we have avoided unwanted consequences.

Amazingly, God does not behave like this. God knew that man would fall into sin and rebellion against him, yet he still carried us through to birth. He did not abort humanity while he carried us in the womb of creation for something that we did not commit, even though He knew we would someday let Him down. He did not abort humanity even though He knew we would disobey Him.

God gave man the freedom necessary to make decisions within his ability. He created man to adequately analyze the given data at a particular place and at a particular time so that he would be liable for the decisions he made. He did not abort us before we could make faulty decisions.

SAFE AND SECURE

When a person asks a Christian, "Why would God create humans and then set them in the garden when he knew they would sin?" our response should be, "Exactly!" That is exactly the right question to ask. This is the generation to unabashedly answer that question. Of course, freedom is the answer. He designed us as beings who would learn to trust Him. He was not afraid to take the risk of creating beings who could make that choice for themselves. Additionally, He did not scrap the whole plan while it was in the making. Consequently, He set an example for humans. He knew ahead of time that we would be tempted to take drastic measures in order to preserve ourselves, even if it meant killing our own offspring while still in the womb. Clearly, God does not behave in this manner. Instead of killing His offspring for something wrong that He knew they would do, He allowed Himself enough room to get involved. God allowed Himself to be inconvenienced by His new creature. He would protect us with His arm.[224] He would shield us as His children.

He protected us because He loved us. Therefore, we should protect others out of love for them. The very essence of protection, as shown by our Creator, involves viewing someone more vulnerable than ourselves as more valuable than ourselves. Protection requires an individual to identify with someone else so deeply, that he is not only willing to fight for him but also take his place.

What does protection have to do with freedom? Some may believe it is obvious why people in society have to protect themselves in order to maintain their liberties. They may say we have to protect ourselves because people can be tempted to be evil and behave badly. Others may disagree with this assessment and say that most people are essentially good.

Although God is in control of all realms, man is given control of his realm, which, first and foremost, is his own person. One has to admit that man is given quite a bit of autonomy within his own realm. If he so chooses, he can destroy himself as well as others. Most reasonable people are not out to destroy themselves or others. Nevertheless, the fact that there are some in this world who are, drives those of us who are not, to take all kinds of precautions. Of course, the extreme form of destruction would be to end human life or to terminate innocence. If we make it through birth, we still have to live in a world that includes criminals: murderers, kidnappers, child molesters, rapists, drug dealers, prostitutes, thieves, and drunk drivers. These groups of people present a high risk to themselves as well as to others. We must protect our friends and families as well as ourselves from these malefactors of society. However, there are still other levels of danger we must face.

It would be foolish for us to think we only needed to protect our friends, families, and selves from hardened criminals. At least two other groups pose dangers. One group that threatens freedom is comprised of individuals who wish to take your property. These individuals pose a medium risk to society. Drunks, drug addicts, shoplifters, pickpockets, computer hackers, identity thieves, car thieves, and burglars can be placed into this category.

The last group poses a lower yet present threat to our society. These include, but are not limited to, intimidators or bullies, chronic liars, cheaters, selfish, inconsiderate, argumentative, divisive and ill-tempered individuals. There are many people who can harm others in different ways. For those who still think that humans are essentially good, they have to admit we live within proximity of people who would harm us simply to get what they want. If some continue to live as though humans are essentially good, they may not have experienced personal injury as a result of unethical behavior. If that is the case, it is most likely a matter of time before they, too, will experience the tarnishing effects of being taken advantage of.

God is a God of life. Although our world is dangerous, life on earth can prove to be a remarkable existence. When we were born into this dangerous, yet amazing environment, we were born into a group of people known as the family. This world provides daily opportunities to work, play, and relax with the people we love.

Family was created for human activity, and we certainly take advantage of it. There are few limits to what we can do. When we are young, our arena of activity is limited to our living room. But as we grow, we want to enjoy the swing set or the swimming pool in the backyard. A child may be satisfied for a few years exploring the backyard. However, after he reaches the ripe old age of five, he is ready to expand his territory. So what does he do? He asks for permission to leave the yard and run over to his friend's house. Mother cringes at the idea of her little baby playing out of her sight, but after phoning his friend's mom, she hesitantly agrees. Once given permission, her child plays with his buddies all day long. He does not want to go home for lunch or dinner.

When a group of children gets together, their list of activities is only limited by their conniving little minds. They can get into all kinds of trouble because dangers, even when limited, are present everywhere. Accidents can certainly happen at home, but parents are confident they can control their domain. The kids wake up, they eat, they play, they nap, they wake up, they play, they eat, they bathe, and after a story they go to bed. This is a crazy time for parents, but it is also the time when parents have the most control over their child's safety. This is an exciting time for children. It is a time of tremendous energy and life. When it is time to close the house for the night, Dad usually checks the doors as part of his nightly routine, making sure that all avenues into the house are tightly locked in order to protect the burgeoning life inside.

Why is this? Chances are that most houses will never be broken into. However, parents faithfully lock the kids in and the burglars out. They do this because it makes them feel safe. They do this because they have a responsibility as parents to make their homes a haven where their kids will not only feel safe, but will indeed be safe. They do this to guard the life they have and the lives they enjoy.

How far are parents willing to go in order to protect their families? Some settle for standard locks on their house. Still others have heavy-duty deadbolts and alarms incorporated into their security measures. However, these measures are still not enough for many folks, so they add a firearm or two. Even in the United States of America, as safe as it is, people go to great lengths in order to protect their families. But where does this obsession with preserving life come from?

We want our families not only to feel safe but to be safe, so we take as many precautions as we can in order to protect them. What is it that we have to protect them from? The answer is simply death. We want to live life to the fullest. In order to live life to the fullest we have to preserve life.

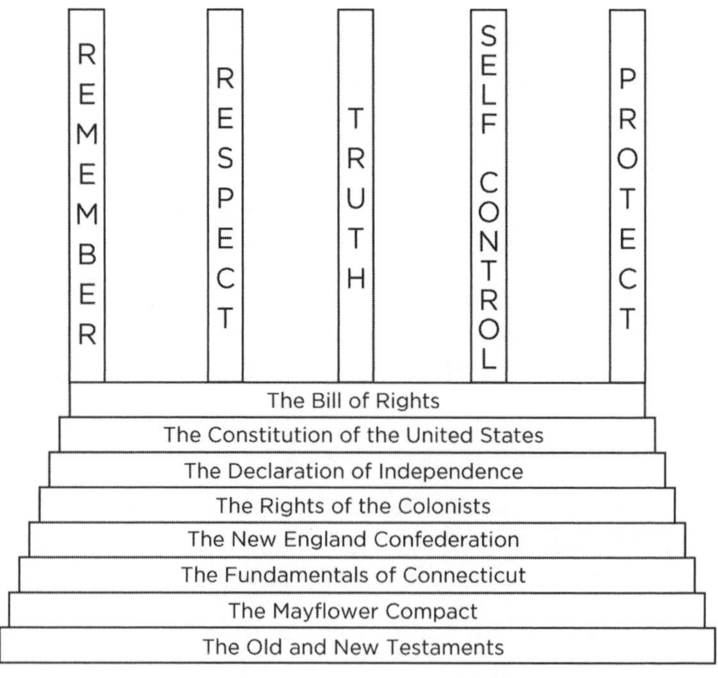

Figure 6 – PROTECT OTHERS

CHAPTER THIRTEEN

The Eternal Fraternity

FLIRTING WITH DEATH OR FLATTERED WITH LIFE

If preserving life is so important, why are most children inclined to push the limits of their activities into the danger zone? This approach to life is a part of the human experience and certainly can assist in healthy growth and development. They can climb trees, jump off their parents' second story balcony into the swimming pool, swing off a rope into a lake, hike mountains, swim in the ocean, rappel down a mountainside, kayak over rapids, experience life to its fullest.

Many adults have the same tendency to live life on the edge. But what exactly is the edge? It is a limitation to what we humans can do with our lives. It is more like a ledge that is thrilling to look over because we realize only a few inches separate us from this life and the next. Some people, such as bungee jumpers, skydivers, mountain climbers, and kayakers, enjoy the thrill of flirting with death and intentionally seek it. Are they flirting with death or flattered with life? Others find themselves placed on the edge accidentally or unintentionally. These people could be parents speeding to work so they will not be late again. A car turns into their path or a deer jumps out in front of them, and before they can yell, "Oh my God!" or "Jesus!" they have either collided with or avoided the collision.

What is it that we are obsessed with? Life. Therefore, we have to protect ourselves from death. It is instinctive. We push our limits, but our limits push back. Our primary limiting factor is not life but death. As we stand over the lifeless body of a friend or loved one in a coffin we make statements such as, "She was so full of life." Why do we say such things? We realize that no matter how much life we experience, one day we still will have it taken away. Nothing can stop death from happening. Sure, we can prevent it for a while, but deep in the crevices of our minds, we know there will come a day when we too will face the cold, when no human will be able to protect us from the icy hand of death.

CONCLUSION

As one delves into what can be known on this planet—about this planet and about the inhabitants of this planet—it is impossible to ignore that God has transmitted light years of information through special revelation. We humans were not intended to discover everything on our own. He assists us. Without His aid we would never know ultimate freedom. Ultimate freedom has to do with the realm of life. What if we could experience life, not just for a time, but for eternity? In fact, we can experience eternal life, but not without a price.

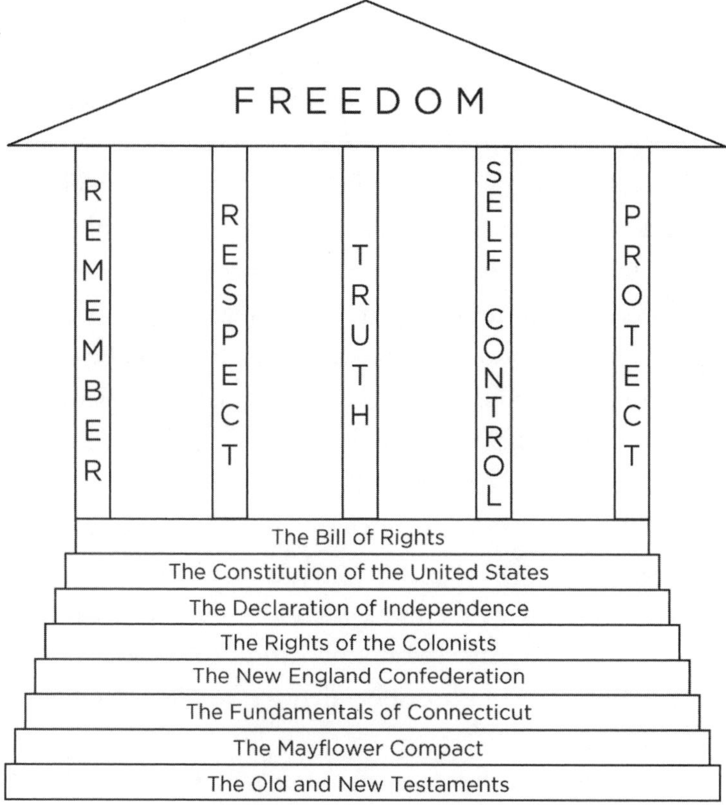

Figure 7 - RESPONSIBILITY PROMOTES FREEDOM

Herein lies the secret to ultimate liberty. In order to be freed from the clutches of death, we must be willing to give up our lives. We know, as dying creatures, that we are eventually going to give up our lives, so why not give them up to gain more life? God provided a way for us to experience eternal life, but it can only be experienced if we sacrifice this life for Him. However, we have to realize we can do nothing to impress an Almighty God. Therefore, no stunt that we can do in this life is going to impress Him.

Then what can we offer to a living God? He has always existed, and His existence is marked by constant, enduring experience. Here lies the folly of offering our experiences to God. We fail to recognize that to use our experiences to barter for His is nothing more than dead men negotiating. First of all, a dead man cannot speak, let alone negotiate. Only a fool would hire a dead man for his physical labor. In the same way, God who is a spiritual being cannot employ a man who is spiritually dead.[225] Not only is man incapable to speak, he cannot relate to or accumulate eternal experiences. Consequently we need someone other than ourselves to bring us forward.

All the good we have to offer God is nothing more than digested food. If food represents that which is good, and a man consumes that which is good, he absorbs the nourishment and the energy that food offers him. All that is left from the exchange is waste. To offer human waste to others is not only unthinkable but horribly offensive; to offer it to God is even worse.

The ancients did not offer that which was processed through their bodies to God as a sacrifice. They were required to take an animal, kill it, and then offer it as a sacrifice on a burning altar. Fire transformed the sacrifice, creating lifelike qualities as the dead sacrifice gave of itself to fuel the flame.

In the same way, an exchange must be made today. We have to give up everything we value, which is really worth nothing because we are going to die anyway. This is painfully obvious to humans. Anything that we can offer to God must be within the realm of time because our lives will fade, and the ultimate destination of our present bodies is the grave. God knows this, and we know it too.

To offer a living God actions in a dying body would demonstrate that we do not really understand the value of life. The essence of life causes dying actions to pale. God desires the action of undying life. This is the act of being; it is an ongoing, undying action that culminates in a living sacrifice.[226] To offer anything less to the undying, ongoing Being is offensive and unproductive.

Therefore, the only thing we can offer to impress God is a view of ourselves that matches His view of us. He wants us to realize that to Him our deaths are worth nothing, but our lives are worth everything. Since we cannot do anything to prevent death, He is willing to take our deaths, but He will only take our deaths if we are willing to give Him our lives. He gave His life that we might have life;[227] we have to give Him our lives that we might have life. Jesus gave up His life in heaven, in order to bring life to earth; we have to give up our lives on earth in order to have life in heaven.[228] The exchange is temporal life for eternal life. Rather than calculating our lives as worth everything to us, we need to value them as nothing in order to gain something that truly is worth everything. Ultimate freedom is achieved when we compare the life we have to the life He has to offer us and realize that eternity is worth more.

God wants to be involved in our lives; do we want to be involved with His? He wants to give us His life; do we want to give Him ours?

Life is a string of experiences. We have one experience after another. We attempt to prolong those experiences and to look for one event that defines us, a climactic achievement. But is that all that we need? The fact that we are never really satisfied with the current experiences must mean that this utopian finale does not exist in this life. All this life has to offer is periodic experiences.

Now steps the Almighty onto stage earth. He plans to really satisfy us, not by offering a series of periodic experiences but rather by offering enduring experience. Enduring experience does not come without a price, and that price is none other than our very lives.

We thrive on experiences. When we have positive experiences, those noticed by men, we take pictures, tape events, and receive trophies. These commemorations prove to be the greatest manifestation of our fleeting lives. They also prove how little our achievements are worth and how far we are willing to go in order to preserve them. If we achieve success, it proves to be a fulfilling experience for a while. But the feeling soon fades and all we have left are a few dated photos and a dusty trophy. What if we could do more than just preserve an experience? What if we could prolong the state of those good experiences for eternity? That is the difference between periodic experiences and an enduring experience. It is also the difference between God's life and ours, God's existence and ours, God's experience and ours.

We collect trophies; God collects people.[229] God has no use for human achievements; God has eternal use for humans. Our trophies mark an experience; God prizes humans. Our trophies are made out of plastic, wood, marble, and metal. God's treasures are conceived in flesh and blood and reborn by the spirit. Our trophies are markers; God's treasures are enduring. Our trophies are given by people; God's treasures are people.

To achieve ultimate liberty in this life, we have to dedicate ourselves to the next life. True freedom is the state of being released from death, and we have the key to release us today. This release is not accomplished by killing ourselves but by giving ourselves. Since we are commissioned as physical beings who are going to die, we have to pursue the experience that will allow us to live. No known antidote is produced by this planet to cure us, so we are victims of our environment. The only cure for death is to look to Someone outside our environment. He is the One who created life in the first place. We are to trust Him that He has the power to do so once again. The realization of these truths produces the necessary faith to transform the death of this life into freedom in the next. This faith is the tiny seed required to remove the mountainous obstacle of death so that we might enjoy, not only freedom in this life, but also in the one to come.

Apart from God we attempt to achieve all that life has to offer. Ironically, in order to achieve the fullness of this life, we must embrace death just as people do who live life on the edge. Those who risk their lives are forced to face the possibility of death. However, it is not until a person has really faced death that he comes to understand the fullness of life. This happens to be the reason so many people who experience near death turn their lives around. They had a defining moment, a moment of truth.

Even if a person realizes that life can only be lived to its fullest by pushing it to the edge of death, he is still forced to live within his limitations. But what if the edge could be taken away? What if there were no limits upon existence? This freedom is exactly what Jesus Christ has made available to us. He came from the other side of the edge, which we refer to as eternity. He brought eternity to us and took the edge of death out of the way. It is now possible to achieve ultimate life beyond the edge. The only requirement is that we must receive the enduring existence He offers in exchange for our limited one.

"For whoever wishes to save his life will lose it; but whoever loses his life for My sake will find it. For what will it profit a man if he gains the whole world and forfeits his soul? Or what will a man give in exchange for his soul?" — Jesus Christ.[230]

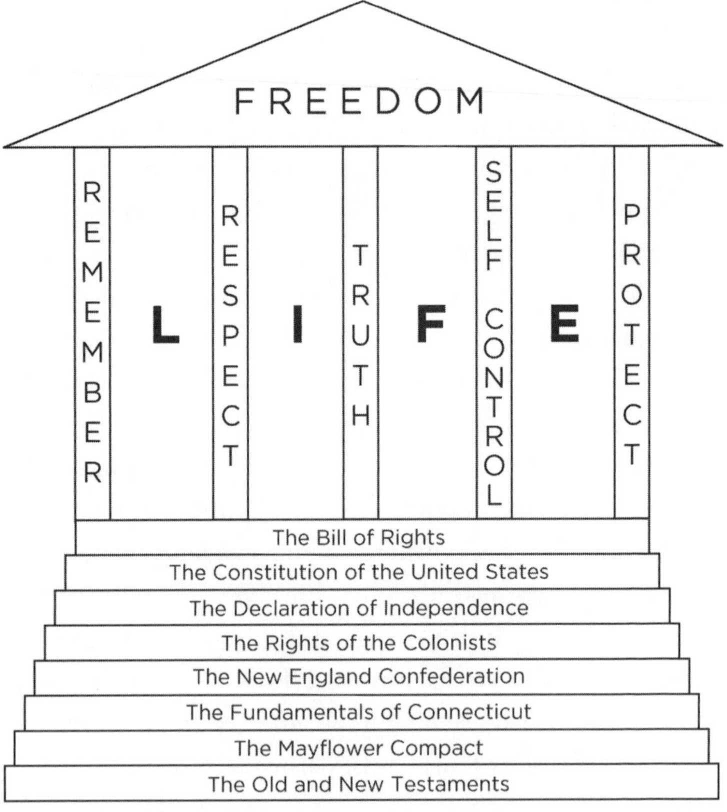

Figure 8 - FREEDOM PRESERVES LIFE

ENDNOTES

1. http://frwebgate.access.gpo.gov/cgi-bin/getpage.cgi?dbname =2003_record&position= all&page=H399.

2. David Herbert Donald, *Lincoln,* (New York: Simon & Schuster, 1995), p. 234.

3. Kathleen Parker, "Eat, drink and Sue", 23 July 2003, http://www.jewishworldreview. com/kathleen/parker072303.asp.

4. C.S. Lewis, *Mere Christianity,* (SanFrancisco: HarperSanFrancisco, 1952), pp. 71 ff.

5. Luke 6:31.

6. Luke 10:33-35.

7. The Declaration of Independence.

8. John Adams, *The Works of John Adams, Second President of the United States,* Charles Francis Adams, ed. (Boston: Little, Brown, 1854), Vol. IX, p. 229, October 11, 1798.

9. http://www.yale.edu/lawweb/avalon/debates/628.htm.

10. Ephesians 4:16.

11. U.S. Constitution.

12. Donald, p. 462.

13. http://www.yale.edu/lawweb/avalon/amerdoc/mayflower.htm.

14. http://www.yale.edu/lawweb/avalon/order.htm.

15. http://www.yale.edu/lawweb/avalon/art1613.htm.

16. *American Patriotism: Speeches, Letters, and Other Papers Which Illustrate the Foundation, The Development, the Preservation of the*

United States of America, Selim H. Peabody, ed. (NY: American Book Exchange, 1880), p. 34.

17. The Declaration of Independence.

18. M. E. Bradford, *A Worthy Company* (NH: Plymouth Rock Foundation, 1982), pp. viii-ix.

19. B. F. Morris, *The Christian Life and Character of the Civil Institutions of the United States* (Philadelphia: George W. Childs, 1864), p.326.

20. Tim LaHaye, *Faith of Our Founding Fathers* (Brentwood, TN: Wolgemuth & Hyatt, Publishers, Inc., 1987), pp. 41-42.

21. Washington, *The Writings of Washington,* Vol. XI, p. 343, May 2, 1778.

22. Thomas Jefferson, *Writings of Thomas Jefferson,* Vol. XV, p. 277, September 28, 1820. http://www.landmarkcases.org/marbury/jefferson.html.

23. David Barton, *Original Intent: The Courts, The Constitution, and Religion,* (Aledo, TX: WallBuilder Press, 2000), p. 272.

24. http://caselaw.lp.findlaw.com/cgi-bin/getcase.pl?court=us&vol=492&invol=573.

25. http://www.broadmanholman.com/article.asp?article=36.

26. http://www.foxnews.com/story/0,2933,119035,00.html
http://www.foxnews.com/story/0,2933,205317,00.html

27. Thomas Jefferson, *Jefferson Writings,* Merrill D. Peterson, ed. (NY: Literary Classics of the United States, Inc., 1984), p. 510, January 1, 1802; see also *Reynolds v. U.S.;* 98 U.S. 164 (1878).

http://caselaw.lp.findlaw.com/cgi-bin/getcase.pl?court=us&vol=98&invol=145.

28. David Barton, *The Myth of Separation,* (Aledo, TX: WallBuilder Press, 1992), p. 42.

29. Barton, p. 147.

30. Tim LaHaye and David Noebel, *Mindsiege*, (Nashville: Word, 2000), p. 188.

31. The American Civil Liberties Union, *Freedom is why we are here,* (www.aclu.org, Fall 1999), pp. 2-4 http://www.aclu.org/FilesPDFs/ACFD11.pdf

32. Barton, p. 148.

33. Donald, 201.

34. Francis A. Schaeffer, *The God who is there,* (Downers Grove: InterVarsity Press, 1968), p. 92-97.

35. Merriam-Webster's Collegiate Dictionary, Tenth Edition (Springfield, Massachusetts: Merriam-Webster, 1993) p. 1269.

36. *A Dictionary of Thoughts: Being a Cyclopedia of Laconic Quotations from the Best Authors of the World, Both Ancient and Modern*, Tryon Edwards, ed. (Detroit, Michigan: F.B. Dickerson co, 1908), p. 589.

37. Schaeffer, p. 23.

38. http://www.cnn.com/US/9811/18/jonestown.anniv.01/.

39. *Star Wars Episode 2: Attack of the Clones,* Dir. George Lucas, (DVD: Lucasfilm, 2002), Ch. 12 (Jedi Archives) 34:31.

40. http://www.allaboutscience.org/darwins-theory-of-evolution.htm.

41. David A. Noebel, J.F. Baldwin and Kevin Bywater, *Clergy in the Classroom,* (Manitou Springs: Summit, 2001), pp. 6, 7, 95, 113, 121, 127.

42. The Associated Press, *Americans: Profanity rampant,* The News and Advance, 29 March 2006, A1, 8.

43. Luke 10:27.

44. 2 Corinthians 10:12.

45. John 15:13.

46. Matthew 5:44.

47. http://www.answersingenesis.org/creation/v18/i2/dogs.asp.

48. Michael J. Behe, PHD makes a similar argument in favor of irreducible complexities by using the example of blood clotting. Behe states, "If your blood hadn't clotted in the right place and in the right amount and at the right time, you would have bled to death. As it turns out, the system of blood clotting involves a highly choreographed cascade of ten steps that use about twenty different molecular components. Without the whole system in place, it doesn't work.... The real trick with blood clotting isn't so much the clot itself – it's just a blob that blocks the flow of blood – but it's the regulation of the system.... How can blood clotting develop over time, step by

step, when in the meantime the animal has no effective way to stop from bleeding to death whenever it's cut? And when you've only got part of a system in place, the system doesn't work, so you've got the components sitting around doing nothing – and natural selection only works if there is something useful right now, not in the future." Lee Strobel, *The Case For A Creator,* (Grand Rapids: Zondervan, 2004), pp. 209-211.

49. Proverbs 1:7.

50. David Barton, *Original Intent: The Courts, The Constitution, and Religion,* (Aledo, TX: WallBuilder Press, 2000), p. 243.

51. J. Kerby Anderson, *Moral Dilemmas,* (Nashville: Word, 1998), p. 59.

52. http://www.cdc.gov/std/HPV/2004HPV%20Report.pdf, p. 8.

53. Strobel, p. 164.

54. 1 Corinthians 6:12.

55. Matthew 22:37-39

56. Genesis 1:1-5.

57. 2 Peter 3:8.

58. Henry M. Morris, *Scientific Creationism,* (El Cajon: Master Books, 1985), p. 223.

59. Romans 14:23; James 1:17; 1 John 1:5-8.

60. 1 Corinthians 14:33, 40.

61. Galatians 2:21.

62. 1 Kings 8:46; Ecclesiastes 7:20.

63. http://www.census.gov/prod/2004pubs/p20-553.pdf, p. 5.

64. Riyad Hermas, *Capitalism is no enemy of Islam,* The News and Advance, 20 May 2006, B1.

65. Ergun Mehmet Caner and Emir Fethi Caner, *Unveiling Islam: An Insider's Look at Muslim Life and Beliefs,* (Grand Rapids: Kregel, 2002), pp. 47-49.

66. Josh McDowell, *The New Evidence That Demands A Verdict,* (Nashville: Thomas Nelson, 1999), p. 38.

67. Psalm 18:30.

68. http://bible-history.com/pontius_pilate/pilateArchaeology.htm. Paul L. Maier, *In the Fullness of Time* (Grand Rapids: Kregel Publications, 1991), pp. 145ff.

69. Matthew 6:9

70. John 14:13, 14.

71. Josh McDowell and Don Stewart, *Handbook of Today's Religions,* (Nashville: Thomas Nelson, 1983), p. 377-99.

72. Caner and Caner pp. 55-62.

73. Genesis 3:15.

74. Genesis 6:8.

75. Genesis 11:7.

76. Isaiah 41:8.

77. Genesis 22:2 ff.

78. Genesis 15:6

79. Genesis 17:7

80. Genesis 17:11.

81. Exodus 12:41.

82. Exodus 12:29.

83. Exodus 12:23.

84. Exodus 14:14ff.

85. Deuteronomy 28:1-68.

86. Deuteronomy 18:15-19.

87. Genesis 4:4.

88. Genesis 3:21.

89. Genesis 2:16, 17.

90. 1 Samuel 9:2.

91. 2 Samuel 7:16.

92. 2 Kings 24:1 – 25:30.

93. Daniel 7:13, 14.

94. Isaiah 53:3-12; 9:1; 14:1; 18:7; 19:21.

95. Jeremiah 31:30-34.

96. Isaiah 14:1; Micah 4:1-5; Zechariah 8:20-23.

97. Romans 7:12, 16.

98. Matthew 5:20; 23:1-4; Romans 4:15; Galatians 2:16; 3:19-23.
99. Matthew 5:17, 18; Galatians 2:21; 3:24.
100. Isaiah 26:9-21; 49:1-7.
101. Psalm 5:4.
102. Romans 4:13-15; 5:12-14, 20, 21; 7:5-25; 8:3; Galatians 2:16.
103. Galatians 3:10-29.
104. Matthew 1:1.
105. Luke 2:42-47.
106. Matthew 14:21; 19:14.
107. Deuteronomy 6:7.
108. Luke 4:1-17.
109. Matthew 7:29; 8:16.
110. Matthew 9:10.
111. Matthew 12:38, 39; 13:2; Luke 8:19-56; John 5:36.
112. Matthew 22:15-46; Luke 20:45-47.
113. John 7:50-53; 19:38-42.
114. Matthew 26:55-68; 27:18-26.
115. John 5:18
116. F.F. Bruce, *New Testament History,* (New York: Doubleday, 1980), pp. 34; 66; 152-153; 164-165; 349.
117. Matthew 11:29.
118. Matthew 22:21.
119. Matthew 26:53; 27:42.
120. John 2:15; 8:7.
121. Matthew 21:14; Luke 15:1ff.; 18:10-15; 19:1-10; John 8:1-11.
122. Mark 4:35-41; John 18:19-24.
123. Galatians 2:20; Philippians 4:13.
124. Romans 6:8-14.
125. 1 Peter 2:23.
126. Galatians 6:17; Hebrews 12:2.
127. Matthew 9:28; Mark 9:23, 24.
128. John 15:5, 7, 11.
129. Matthew 28:18-20; Mark 16:15.
130. Luke 6:27; 1 Peter 4:8.

131. 1 John 4:7-12.

132. John 15:13; Romans 5:6-11.

133. John 7:24

134. Donald, p.81.

135. The Associated Press, *Americans: Profanity rampant,* The News and Advance, 29 March 2006, A1, 8.

136. Linda Marsa, *Tattoos, piercings may signify trouble, study finds,* Los Angeles Times, 17 September 2002.

137. Luke 13:1-5

138. Luke 10:25-37

139. Genesis 1:27

140. 1 Peter 3:7; 1 John 4:7,8,19-21.

141. Scott Hyland, *Christian Ethics, The Popular Encyclopedia of Apologetics: Surveying the Evidence for the Truth of Christianity,* Ed Hindson and Ergun Caner, ed. (Eugene, Oregon: Harvest House, 2008), p. 201.

142. Romans 5:12.

143. John 1:15; 17:5; Hebrews 7:3.

144. Philippians 2:6, 7.

145. John 10:18.

146. Matthew 5:16; John 12:20-50; 13:31, 32; 17:1-5.

147. Philippians 2:8; Matthew 26:38, 39.

148. John 6:35-40.

149. Romans 5:12-21.

150. Genesis 2:16, 17.

151. Romans 5:18.

152. 2 Corinthians 5:21.

153. Matthew 27:52, 53.

154. Hebrews 7:26.

155. Genesis 4:10, Hebrews 12:24.

156. 2 Corinthians 5:21.

157. Romans 5:6-11, 6:6; Hebrews 7:27, 10:10; 1 Peter 3:18.

158. Romans 4:24, 5:18-6:11; Galatians 1:1.

159. Matthew 20:28; Ephesians 5:2.

160. John 14:20; 17:19-26 .

161. Romans 4:25; 1 Corinthians 15:20-28; 2 Corinthians 5:1-19.

162. Galatians 2:20.

163. Schaeffer, p. 88.

164. Matthew 1:23.

165. Judges 13:22; Isaiah 6:5.

166. Matthew 3:16, 17; 28:19; John 5:18; 14:15-21.

167. 1 John 4:20.

168. 1 Peter 3:7

169. Matthew 6:12-15.

170. John 1:1-18; Colossians 1:15-20; Hebrews 1:1-4.

171. James 1:17; 1 John 1:5-8.

172. 1 John 2:8-11.

173. John 8:12.

174. John 8:44; 1 Peter 5:8.

175. 2 Corinthians 4:4; Colossians 1:15; Hebrews 1:3.

176. Genesis 1:26; 5:1; 1 Corinthians 11:7.

177. Jeremiah 31:33; Ezekiel 36:26, 27.

178. John 1ff.; Colossians 1ff.; Hebrews 1ff..

179. Galatians 4:4.

180. John 8:12

181. Acts 17:28; 1 Corinthians 15:28; Ephesians 1:23; Colossians 3:11.

182. Matthew 20:28; John 8:32.

183. Psalm 139:1-16.

184. Luke 12:48; 19:17.

185. Genesis 39:9.

186. 2 Corinthians 2:6-8.

187. Genesis 45:5, 50:20.

188. Luke 10:27, 28.

189. 1 John 4:19.

190. Matthew 10:23; John 15:13

191. Martin Niemoller, *German Protestant pastor,* 1892-1984, (Yad Vashem, The Martyrs' and Heroes' Remembrance Authority P.O.B. 3477 Jerusalem 91034 Israel, 5 January, 1997).

192. Genesis 1:26.

193. Genesis 2:7.

194. Genesis 2:21-23.

195. Genesis 2:24.

196. 1 Corinthians 11:7-12.

197. Genesis 1:28.

198. Ephesians 5:28.

199. Hebrews 13:4.

200. 1 Timothy 3:4, 5.

201. 1 Timothy 5:8.

202. Robert L. Woodson Sr., *Reducing Poverty: The Joseph Principle,* (Grove City: Vision & Values, October 2005), Vol. 13 No. 2 pp.1-3.

203. Genesis 1:28.

204. 1 Corinthians 7:1.

205. Exodus 22:16, 17; Deuteronomy 22:28, 29.

206. 1 Timothy 5:8.

207. Hebrews 13:4.

208. Dr. James Dobson, *Bringing up Boys,* (Wheaton: Tyndale, 2001), pp. 124-126.

209. Anderson, pp. 149-151.

210. Matthew 19:12.

211. Barbara Downs, *Fertility of American Women: June 2002,* U.S. Census Department Current Population Reports, P20-548. US Census Bureau, Washington, DC (2003), p. 1, 3. Archived at: http://www.census.gov/prod/2003pubs/p20-548.pdf.

212. http://www.plannedparenthood.org/pp2/portal/files/portal/medicalinfo/birthcontrol/ bio-margaret-sanger.xml. http://womenshistory.about.com/library/bio/blbio_margaret_sanger.htm.

213. Genesis 1:27-29.

214. Leviticus 15:16-18.

215. Dr. James Dobson, *Bringing up Girls,* (Carol Stream: Tyndale, 2010), pp. 37, 38.

216. Genesis 3:6.

217. Exodus 22:16, 17.

218. Ephesians 5:28, 29.
219. Proverbs 5:15-20.
220. 1 Timothy 2:15; Titus 2:4, 5.
221. Song of Solomon 4:7-15.
222. 1 Peter 3:1-6.
223. Dobson, *Bringing up Girls,* 115-119.
224. Isaiah 52:10-15.
225. 1 Corinthians 15:42-57.
226. Romans 12:1.
227. 1 Corinthians 15:45.
228. 1 Corinthians 15:53-55.
229. 2 Corinthians 12:14, 15.
230. Matthew 16:25, 26.

INDEX